D1557719

The wee cookbook

BLESSED ARE THE PEACEMAKERS
FOR THEY WILL BE CALLED THE
CHILDREN OF GOD.

MATTHEW 5:9

Copyright © 1983

THE IRISH CHILDREN'S FUND

First Printing	January, 1983	2,000 copies
Second Printing	May, 1983	2,000 copies
Third Printing	January, 1984	6,000 copies
Fourth Printing	February, 1985	10,000 copies

ISBN 0-9614331-2-4

Additional copies may be ordered from THE IRISH CHILDREN'S FUND, 5602 Hillcrest Road, Downers Grove, IL 60516. Please send $7.95 plus $1.00 postage and handling for each copy. Illinois residents add $.50 tax.

KANSAS CITY PRESS, INC.

THE COOKBOOK PEOPLE

Olathe, Kansas
800/821-5745

The Irish Children's Fund wishes to thank its host families and their friends for contributing their favorite recipes to "The Wee Cookbook".

The ICF was organized to help break the cycle of bitterness and hate in which many of Northern Ireland's young people find themselves today. Youngsters from the war-torn areas of Belfast and Derry stay with American host families for the summer. The families raise the money for air fare and insurance through grassroots fund raising.

Proceeds from the sale of "The Wee Cookbook" also go towards a follow-up program for the children in Northern Ireland. This phase consists of weekend get-togethers for the children to help break down the barriers of misunderstanding that exist between them. If you would care for more information on the ICF please write us at 5602 Hillcrest Rd., Downers Grove, IL 60516 or call (312) 968-6275.

To those who have purchased "The Wee Cookbook" we wish you every enjoyment with the recipes and the Lord's richest blessing upon you.

Artwork donated by Nancy Suffolk

TABLE OF CONTENTS

IRISH RECIPES

A Taste of Irish Excellence

The Irish Culinary Team was the proud winner of a Bronze Medal at the 1984 World Culinary Olympics which were held in Frankfurt, West Germany. They took the honors in the hot food division, the most prestigious event in the entire competition. More than 1,000 chefs from 28 countries competed and 70,000 visitors from 50 nations attended the Olympics.

That old cliche about Irish food being bland and tasteless has been refuted once and for all. Irish cuisine has come of age and the chefs in Ireland today are among the best in the world.

We congratulate the Irish Culinary Team on their victory. They are as follows: Noel Cullen (Team Captain), John Coughlan (Secretary), Eugene McGovern (Manager), Brendan O'Neill, John Morrin, Joe Erraught, Gerald Moore, Joe Scanlon, Noel McHugh, and Gunter Hoffman.

In this special section of The Wee Cookbook we are privileged to publish exclusively, the Bronze Medal recipes.

Baked Liffey Salmon Grainne

4		5 oz. salmon fillets	2	T	lemon juice
8	oz.	spinach leaves	salt and pepper		
6	oz.	Dublin Bay prawns	8	oz.	puff pastry
3	oz.	butter	½		bottle white wine
½	pt.	cream	1		clove garlic
pinch of dill for marinade			nutmeg		

Prepare salmon into fillets, set to marinate in wine, dill, herbs for approximately 3 hours. Blanch spinach with garlic, seasoning and nutmeg—cool quickly to return color. Make filling for salmon by mincing cooked prawns. Add lemon juice, butter, cream and blend in blender. Make pocket in salmon and fill with prawn mixture — wrap the salmon in spinach leaves and finally wrap in puff pastry. Make into fish shape. Make an opening (about ½") in top of pastry. Bake for 17 minutes at 300 degrees. When cooked fill the opening in the pastry with mousseline sauce.

Mousseline Sauce:

8		eggs	⅓	pt.	cream (semi-whipped)
1	#	butter (unsalted)	1	T	lemon juice
6	oz.	vinegar	bay leaf		
		(tarragon or white wine vinegar)	peppercorns		
			salt & pepper		

Make reductions to ⅓ of volume; vinegar, lemon juice, bay leaf and peppercorns. Separate eggs and add yolks to reduction, beat vigorously over gentle heat to ribbon state and add butter. Finally add cream and correct seasoning. 4 portions.

-

Escalope of Veal Sceilig

4		5 oz. escalope (slices) of veal	½	oz.	red lump roe
4	oz.	cooked crab meat	½	pt.	fish stock
4	oz.	pork fat	4	oz.	butter
4	oz.	minced lean veal	1	t	chopped chives
1		egg white	½		glass white wine
½	pt.	cream	1		whole egg for batter
1		clove garlic			

Prepare sliced veal into escalope (5 oz. each). Prepare mousseline force-meat (finely minced); quantities of 4 oz. minced lean veal, 4 oz. pork fat, 4 oz. crabmeat, 1 egg white and ½ pt. cream. Make reduction of white wine and seasonings and reduce to about 2 tablespoons. Let cool. Mix the force-meat and wine reduction in a blender till soft (consistency of soft whipped cream. Add red lump roe to mousseline and place into each escalope. Fold escalopes and seal. Season escalopes and dip in egg and cream mixture (equal quantities). Set to cook in hot oil and brown on both sides. Remove to finish in moderate oven for 20 minutes till done. Serve sliced on bed of sauce.

Sauce: Prepare and cook fish stock; white wine, herbs, white vegetables (onions, turnips, etc.) and white fish bones for 20 minutes. Strain and reduce to glaze. Add chopped chives and add 4 oz. butter. Serve sauce under veal. 4 portions.

Breast of Guinea Fowl Aisling

2		2½ lbs. each guinea fowl	1	t	parsley
6	oz.	pork fat	3	oz.	Irish Mist
4	oz.	smoked bacon	6	oz.	butter
2		eggs	12	oz.	mixed root vegetables (aromates)
½	pt.	cream	milled pepper		

Bone guinea fowl. Remove breast. Remove meat from legs. Marinate both meats in mixture of meade (Irish whiskey), mixed root vegetables, herbs and oil. Prepare farce (finely minced mixture) for breast; 6 oz. pork fat, 4 oz. smoked bacon, leg meat of guinea fowl, 2 egg whites, ½ pt. cream, seasonings and chopped parsley. Trim and prepare breast of guinea fowl with skin on. Remove inner fillet, beat out fillet, make pocket in breast. Place farce into pocket, cover with fillet and make cylindrical shape. Make stock from guinea fowl bones — reduce stock to glaze. Make a mixture with glaze, 3 oz. Irish Mist and 6 oz. melted butter. Brush the guinea fowl breast with this mixture and shape and wrap in tinfoil. Cook on trivet of vegetables for approximately 20 minutes. Slice and serve with gold colored frill.

Sauce:

4	oz.	redcurrants	dash Grenadine
½	pt.	cream	½ pt. demi-glaze
4	oz.	Irish Mist	

Cook redcurrants, cream, Irish Mist and glaze. Correct seasoning and color with Grenadine, liquidize and strain. Serve sauce under guinea fowl. Garnish with watercress or mustard cress. 4 portions.

Tomato Flavored Potatoes

8   medium potatoes
2   tomatoes
1 oz. finely diced onion
pinch of oregano
chopped parsley
cooking oil
seasoning

Shape potatoes to chateau shape with flat surface on one side. Prepare hollow in center of potato with parisienne spoon, slice each end of the potato thinly without cutting right through. Set to roast on tray in hot oven, 10-15 minutes or till soft. Skin and de-seed tomatoes and cook with oregano and pinch of finely diced onion and parsley. When potatoes are cooked, fill the hollow with tomato mixture and brush with butter. Serve with tiny fennel leaf.

Red Cabbage Parcel

1		head red cabbage
2		apples
6	oz.	cider
1	#	bacon (sliced)
1		spice bag
4	oz.	butter

Select large outer leaves of cabbage — retain. Shred heart of cabbage, apples and dice 2 oz. of bacon. Blanch and refresh outer leaves, allow to cool. Braise the shredded cabbage, apple, and diced bacon with cider. Add spice bag. Extract cooking liquor. Place the braised cabbage mixture into the outer leaves and roll up. Roll the remaining sliced bacon around each cabbage bundle, about 2 slices per bundle, and place onto braising pan. Cover with the extracted cooking liquor and cook in moderate oven approximately 20 minutes. Brush with clarified butter.

Spinach Parcel

8 oz. large leaf spinach
8 oz. finely diced vegetables (carrot, leek, celery)
4 oz. Jigginstown cheese, grated (Gruyere)
1   beaten egg
salt & pepper
grated nutmeg

Blanch and refresh spinach, dry and lay-out flat leaves on some cling film. Season and dust with nutmeg. Dice vegetables very fine, blanch and refresh. Grate cheese and add to the diced vegetable. Bind with a beaten egg, season, place mix on spinach leaves, roll in cling film, then in tinfoil, bake for approximately 5 minutes or till warm in a medium oven. Remove from wrappings, slice and serve. Makes about 4 parcels.

Potato Nests

4		large potatoes
2	oz.	flour
6	oz.	pine nuts
3		egg yolks

Prepare and make duchesse potatoes forming same into small potato ball shapes. Toast pine nuts and chop when cool. Dip potato balls into flour, then eggwash, then chopped pine nuts. Make nest shape and deep fry. Fill with redcurrants.

"CHAMP" THE SPUD OF LIFE

In austere times like these one has to make do with less expensive meals, particularly cuts of meats. Therefore, back to the glorious SPUD! The potato is packed with vitamins & minerals & it is somewhat due to the potato that we in Ireland produced strong handsome men & women.

Peel & boil 8 potatoes. Drain & mash with butter, salt & pepper to taste. Chop onions, parsley & some thyme & add to mashed potatoes & bring to a creamy steaming finish. Serve on a large plate in a mound. Make a well in center & pour in melted butter. Each person serves himself some potatoes & butter.

Carmel Quinn
New Jersey

COLCANNON

1 # kale or cabbage
1 # potatoes
2   small leeks or green onions, chopped
¾ c milk or cream
salt, pepper, pinch of mace
½ c butter melted

Cook kale or cabbage just till tender. Cook potatoes till tender. Simmer leeks in milk till soft, about 5 min. Drain potatoes, season with salt, pepper & mace & beat till fluffy. Add leeks & milk, place over low heat & blend in kale, beat till mixture is a pale green fluff. Spoon into warm bowl, making a well in center. Pour in melted butter to fill well. Leftovers are good fried in hot bacon fat till crisp & brown on both sides.

Sharon Zieman
Downers Grove

POTATO PANCAKES

2   c freshly mashed potatoes, cooled
1   egg
2   c flour
salt to taste
4   T butter
2   T oil

Mix egg & potatoes with fork. Add 1½ c flour & salt. Mix well with hands. Turn onto floured board, mix in remaining flour to consistency of biscuit dough. Pat out to ¼", or use a rolling pin. Cut into 3" squares. Melt butter & oil in skillet & brown on both sides. Serve with butter.

Mary Ellen Durbin
Lisle

POTATO PANCAKES WITH CHIVES

2		eggs, slightly beaten
1	c	milk
2	T	melted butter
2	c	grated raw potatoes
1	c	pancake mix
2	T	minced chives

Combine egg, milk, butter & potatoes. Stir in pancake mix & chives. Pour ¼ c batter for each pancake into a buttered frying pan. Cook slowly, turning once, till well browned & crisp on both sides. Serve with applesauce if desired.

Diane O'Connor
Downers Grove

BUBBLE & SQUEAK

This dish is named for the noise it makes in the skillet as it cooks.

3 T butter
1   small onion
2 c shredded cooked cabbage
2 c leftover mashed potatoes

Saute onions in butter till tender. Combine cabbage & mashed potatoes. Add to skillet & press with fork to form large cake. Cook over moderate heat till well browned. Loosen potato cake with spatula, slide onto plate & flip back into skillet so that uncooked side is down. Cook till browned. Serve this cut into wedges.

Bonnie Lovison
Chicago

CREAMY POTATO SOUP

¼ c butter
2 medium onions, chopped
2 # red potatoes, peeled & sliced
3 c milk
3 c chicken stock

Melt butter in dutch oven & add onions, cook slowly till tender but not brown. Add potatoes & milk & stock. Cover and cook over low heat till potatoes are tender, about 1 hour. Cool slightly & put soup through sieve or in food processor & puree. Reheat to serving temperature. Season with salt & pepper.

Donna Farrell
Naperville

OUTSTANDING POTATO SOUP

4	T	bacon drippings, or shortening
4	c	peeled raw potatoes, cubed
½	c	chopped parsley
1	c	minced onion
1½	t	salt
½	t	pepper
5	c	College Inn chicken stock
2	c	half & half
4	T	flour
1	c	grated raw carrots

Melt shortening & saute potatoes, parsley, onion, 1 bay leaf, salt & pepper over medium heat. Then cook covered 15-20 min. over low heat. Add chicken stock & cook 15 min. Mix half & half with flour & stir into soup. Keep stirring so no lumps form. Simmer soup for at least 30 min. Put grated carrots in & cook 5 more min. Serve.

Diane O'Connor
Downers Grove

SHEPHERD'S PIE

1   #   potatoes
½   c   beef stock
1   #   cooked, minced beef (leftover roast beef cut in small cubes or
        ground)
2   tomatoes, chopped
1   small onion, chopped
2   T   butter
1   egg, beaten
salt & pepper

Peel & cube potatoes, cook, drain & mash. Saute onions in butter, then crumble in meat & stir in. Add tomatoes, stock & seasonings. Turn mixture into casserole & top with mashed potatoes. Brush top with a little beaten egg & bake at 350° for 20 min. (Almost any leftover vegetables can be added if you wish. You can also top the pie with cooked, sliced potatoes rather than mashed. Use your imagination & your leftovers to create your own version.)

Mildred King
Iowa

"TOAD IN THE HOLE"
Rob's Absolute All-Time Favorite Irish Recipe

1	#	sausage, bulk or links (pork)
12		rounded T flour
8		eggs
4		pinches salt

enough milk to make a thin batter

Bake sausages in a 9x13 glass pan (crumble the bulk or slice the links). Do not drain & if there isn't enough grease to lightly cover the bottom add a little oil & reheat. Beat eggs in one bowl. In another bowl, mix flour & salt. Make a well in flour & add eggs. Beat with a whisk while adding enough milk to make the batter the consistency of cream. Pour batter over hot sausages & bake at 425° for 15-30 min. or till puffed, crispy looking & browned. Serve immediately.

Diane O'Connor
Downers Grove

ULSTER FRY

Ingredients per person:

2	**pieces regular bacon, Irish bacon or Canadian**
2	**regular sausages or Irish sausages**
1	**egg**
2	**slices potato bread**
1	**tomato**

Heat 2 oz. fat in frying pan. Fry sausages first & add bacon. When cooked remove from pan & keep warm in oven. Increase heat & place potato bread & quartered tomato in pan. Cook both sides for approximately 2 min. Lower heat & gently fry egg for about 3 min.

Caroline Cracroft
British Consulate, Chicago

CHUMP STEAK PADDY

1-1½ # chump steak (sirloin or similar)
4   medium potatoes
2   oz. grated cheese
1 t dry mustard
1   8 oz. can tomato sauce
oil, or butter, salt & pepper
chopped parsley

Boil potatoes slowly & then slice thinly. Cut steak into 4 portions. Mix mustard with cheese. Heat oil in frying pan & cook steaks 2-3 minutes on each side till brown. Season & spread each steak with tomato sauce & place in a shallow baking dish. Cover with sliced potatoes & sprinkle mustard mixture on top. Place under broiler till cheese becomes golden. Sprinkle with parsley & serve.

Caroline Cracroft
British Consulate, Chicago

LAMB (MUTTON) PIES

9   c   flour
3   t   baking powder
¼   #   butter
2   t   salt
1   c   milk, or less

Meat: Leg of lamb or lamb shoulder (3½ #), cut in cubes. Make soup of lamb bones, add 2 cans of scotch broth towards end of cooking time.

Sift flour, baking powder & salt. Blend in butter & enough milk to make stiff dough. Knead. Roll out like pie crust, into 8" circle about the size of small saucers. (2 circles for each pie, recipe makes 12 pies.) Place raw meat cubes on pastry, add salt & pepper, put other pastry on top & pinch well all around. Bake at 350° till golden, 40-45 min. Can serve plain or in soup bowls, with ladles of soup over pies. May also be made & refrigerated or frozen, then heated in oven.

Mary Ellen Durbin
Lisle

IRISH STEW

2	#	lamb
1	#	onions
4		stalks celery
1		leek
½	#	carrots
2		oz. barley
1½	#	potatoes
¾		pint cold water

Cut meat into 1" cubes. Season well with salt & pepper. Slice onions thinly & other vegetables thickly. Pack alternate layers of vegetables, barley & meat in ovenproof casserole. Start with onions and end with potatoes. Pour water over, cover & cook 1½-2 hours at 325°. Baste with juices from time to time. Raise oven temp. to 425°, uncover, & brown potatoes.

Donna Doherty
Merrillville, Ind.

PORK & APPLE STEW

6   shoulder pork chops
4   medium cooking apples
3   onions
1½ T brown sugar
1   T water
salt & pepper

Trim chops of excess fat & cut fat into thin strips. Peel, core & slice apples. Slice onions thinly. Put a layer of onions in a casserole, a layer of apples, ½ the brown sugar & the water, the chops, salt & pepper. Cover chops with another layer of onions & top with sliced apples. Lay the strips of fat, criss-cross on top & sprinkle with remaining sugar. Season again with salt & pepper. Cover and cook at 350° for 1 hour, reduce heat & cook another hour if necessary, for meat to be sufficiently cooked.

Maribeth Clingman's cousin in Ireland
Downers Grove

COCK-A-LEEKIE SOUP

½   c   **pearl barley**
2-3 #   **chicken**
1   **veal knuckle (¾ #)**
2   **qts. water**
2   t   **salt**
1   **bay leaf**
6   **peppercorns**
3   **sprigs parsley**
6   **leeks (about 1 #)**

Cover barley with cold water & soak 12 hours. Combine chicken, veal knuckle, water & salt in large pot. Tie bay leaf, peppercorns, & parsley in cheesecloth & add to pot. Drain barley & add to other ingredients, bring to boil over high heat, skim foam. Reduce heat to medium & cook for 1½ hours. Clean & slice leeks & add to soup. Remove chicken & take meat off & return meat to soup. Take out knuckle & discard, also cheesecloth bag. Taste soup & add salt & pepper if necessary.

Bonnie Lovison
Chicago

YORKSHIRE PUDDING

1¾ c **flour**
1 t **salt**
2 **eggs**
2 c **milk**
1 **oz. bacon drippings or lard or oil**

Measure flour & salt in bowl. Make a well in center & break in eggs. Stir gradually, cutting in flour from sides. Stir in milk, a little at a time till a smooth thick batter is formed. Beat till it bubbles. Add remaining milk & set aside 1 hour. Get drippings sizzling hot in 4x5 baking pan or loaf pan. Beat batter again & pour into hot pan. Bake at 475° till nicely browned, about 15 min. Cut into sections & serve on plate with roast beef & gravy.

Sharon Zieman
Downers Grove

GOOD FRIDAY HOT CROSS BUNS

Dissolve 1 pkg. yeast in ¼ c warm water, let stand till bubbly. Heat 1 c buttermilk to lukewarm. Add 2 T sugar, ¼ t baking soda, 1 t each salt & cinnamon, dissolved yeast and ⅓ c shortening. Blend well.

Stir in about 1 c flour & mix well. Stir in ⅔ c raisins & stir in about 2¼ c more flour till dough forms. Turn out on floured surface & knead till smooth & elastic. Put into greased bowl, cover & let rise till double.

Turn out onto floured board, divide & shape dough into 18 balls. Put onto buttered baking sheet. Let rise covered in warm place till double. Bake at 375° for 20 min. Cool on wire rack & drizzle with a thin powdered sugar icing in a cross shape. (In Rob's house in Dublin, these buns were traditionally served on Good Friday.)

Clare Stephens
Dalkey, Co. Dublin

IRISH CHRISTMAS CAKE

2	c	butter		½	c	ground almonds
2	c	sugar		¾	c	whole almonds
8		well-beaten eggs		1		15 oz. pkg. raisins
½	c	brandy (opt.)		3	c	currants
1	T	rose water (opt.)		¾	c	candied cherries
1	t	orange extract		½	c	chop. lemon peel
4	c	flour		½	c	chop. orange peel
2	t	ground allspice				(candied peels)
1	t	salt				

Cream butter & sugar, add eggs, brandy, rose water & orange extract & beat till fluffy. Sift flour, allspice & salt. Stir in ground almonds & stir flour mixture into creamed mixture. Stir in whole almonds, fruits & peels. Grease 10" springform pan (tube type) & place on baking sheet. Pour batter into pan & bake at 300° for 2-2½ hrs. Cool in pan on rack. Remove sides from pan & cool removed cake on rack. Frost with almond paste: Place ½ of an 8 oz. can of almond paste in layers of waxed paper & roll ⅛" thick. Press pieces against side of half the cake, repeat with second half of can. Roll another 8 oz. can of almond paste to a 10" circle, ⅛" thick, cut center away, & place circle on top of cake. Pat sides & top together.

Finally, frost with Royal Icing: In small mixer bowl, combine 3 egg whites (room temp.), 1 1# pkg. powdered sugar, ½ t cream of tartar, & 1 t vanilla. Beat till very stiff. Frost cake immediately because frosting gets very hard. Wrap cake well in tightly covered wrapping or container.

Maeve O'Connor
Blackrock, Co. Dublin

BRAN SCONES

1½	c	whole wheat flour
3	t	baking powder
½	c	bran
1		oz. butter (2 T)
½	c	brown sugar
5		oz. milk

pinch of salt

Mix all dry ingredients. Rub in butter till crumbly. Add milk to form soft dough. Pat out and cut into small wedges. Bake on lightly greased cookie sheet at 450° for 10-12 min.

Frances O'Connor
Killiney, Co. Dublin

IRISH SCONES

6   c   flour
4   regular teaspoons (not measuring teaspoon)
baking powder — heaped
pinch salt
¼   c   sugar
1   stick margarine

Sift flour, powder & salt, add sugar. Add margarine & work in till crumbly. Beat eggs in bowl & add milk to make 2 cups. Add liquid to dry ingredients & mix with spoon till right consistency for kneading. Knead lightly. Roll out & cut with biscuit cutter or cut into wedges. Place on greased cookie sheet, bake at 450° for 10-20 min. or till browned. Can add shredded cheese to batter. Also can be rolled out & sprinkled with nuts, brown sugar & cinnamon, rolled up, cut into spirals & then baked.

Elva O'Connor
Sault St. Marie, Canada

IRISH BRACK

1 # mixed dried fruit (raisins, golden raisins, & currants)
1 c cold tea
1 T black treacle (molasses)
1 c brown sugar
2 c self-raising flour
1 beaten egg

Overnight steep fruit, tea, molasses & sugar. Next day add flour & beaten egg. Place in well oiled loaf tin (2 # size). Bake for 1-1½ hours at 350°. Cool, slice & butter.

A golden ring is usually put into the dough & the lucky recipient is said to be married within the year.

Caroline Cracroft
British Consulate, Chicago

WHEATON BREAD

2   c   whole wheat flour
¾   c   unbleached flour
¼   c   wheat germ or bran
2   T   butter
1   t   sugar
1   t   baking soda
1   t   salt
¼   t   cream of tartar
½   pint buttermilk

Mix all ingredients together. Rub in butter & mix in enough buttermilk to make a soft kneading consistency. Bake in an oiled, floured loaf tin at 350° for 40-45 min.

Emer Torpey
Dalkey, Co. Dublin

PORTER CAKE

1   # flour
1   # golden raisins
½   # raisins
2   t mixed spice
1   t baking soda
½   bottle Guinness
¼   # mixed candied peel
grated lemon rind
1½ c brown sugar
2   sticks butter
4   eggs

Mix butter & flour with fingers till crumbly. Add all dry ingredients.
Heat Guinness with baking soda. Beat eggs & then add to Guinness. Add
this mixture to cake mixture. Bake at 350° to start with, reduce to 325°
& cook for about 3 hours.

Caroline Cracroft
British Consulate, Chicago

IRISH TEA CAKE

2   T   Irish Mist Liqueur
1   c   raisins
¾   c   butter
¾   c   firmly packed brown sugar
3   eggs
2   c   flour
pinch of salt
1   t   baking powder

Add raisins to liqueur & let stand. Cream butter & sugar till fluffy. Add eggs one at a time with 1 t flour, beat till smooth after each addition. Sift remaining flour, powder & salt. Beat into egg mixture. Stir in raisins & liqueur. Pour into 8x4 loaf pan, buttered & lined with buttered wax paper. Bake at 325° for 45 minutes or till loaf tests done. Remove from pan & cool.

Donna Farrell
Naperville

MARY O'DRISCOLL'S BROWN BREAD
From Cobh, Ireland

1		egg
½	#	plain white flour
¾	#	whole wheat flour
1		oz. bran
1		oz. margarine
3	t	sugar

1 rounded t baking soda & salt
½   pint sour milk

Blend margarine with flours & bran. Add sugar, salt, & soda. Break in the egg & add milk. Place in well greased round cake tin. Bake at 300° in center of oven for 25-30 min. Check at 15 min. & when brown tap for doneness (will make hollow sound).

Agnes Limacher & Susan Jary
Joliet

IRISH SODA BREAD

3 c flour
⅔ c sugar
1 T baking powder
1 t baking soda
1 t salt
1½ c raisins
2 beaten eggs
1¾ c buttermilk
2 T melted butter

Sift dry ingredients, stir in raisins. Combine eggs, buttermilk & melted butter. Stir all ingredients by hand till well mixed. Grease 2 9" loaf pans or 1 large loaf pan. Pour in batter & bake at 350° for 1 hr. Remove from pan & cool.

Loni Kelly
South Holland

MAUREEN'S SODA BREAD
WITH CARAWAY SEEDS

2	c	flour
2	T	sugar
2	t	baking powder
1	t	baking soda
½	t	salt
½	c	raisins
1	T	caraway seeds
1	c	buttermilk
3	T	butter

Sift dry ingredients, add raisins & seeds. Cut in butter with hands till mixture crumbly. Add buttermilk & stir quickly with fork just till moistened. Gather up & lightly knead on floured surface for 1 min. Do not work too much. Shape into a ball & place on a greased cookie sheet. Flatten into a 7" circle. With a floured knife cut a cross into the top. Bake at 375° for 30-40 min. or until loaf sounds hollow when tapped. Brush with melted butter if desired.

Diane O'Connor
Downers Grove

IRISH SODA FARLS

Sift ½ # of plain flour, add a level t of baking soda, ¼ t salt & stir in a ¼ pint of buttermilk or sour milk. Mix till the dough is soft. Knead very lightly. Turn out onto a floured board & shape into a round about ½" thick. Cut into quarters. Bake on a floured griddle for 10-15 min.

Agnes Limacher & Susan Jary
Joliet

IRISH POTATO BREAD

Mix 8 oz. of mashed potatoes, a t salt, 1 or 2 oz. of butter & sufficient flour with a little milk to make a stiff dough. Roll out to ¼" thick & cut into 8 pieces. Cook on a griddle browning on both sides, & prick with fork. Can also use for breakfast, fried in bacon fat with bacon & eggs.

Mary Ann O'Brien
Frankfort

ARMAGH APPLE GRIDDLE CAKE

1 # cooked potatoes
1 t salt
4 T flour
1 oz. butter
1 # cooking apples
sugar to taste
knob of butter
2 cloves (optional)

Mash potatoes with butter & salt, work in flour & divide mixture in half & roll each part into a round. Chop apples, add sugar & butter & spread on 1 round. Top with other round, seal well. Bake both sides on a well-heated griddle (or frying pan). By tradition the sugar & butter should be omitted in the apple mixture & added on serving, by splitting the cake across the top & lifting the lid.

Caroline Cracroft
British Consulate, Chicago

STUFFED BAKED APPLES

4		baking apples (Rome Beauties or Greening)
½	c	prepared mincemeat
1	c	apple cider
2	T	butter or margarine

Wash and core apples. Pare upper half of each apple to prevent splitting. Place apples upright in small baking dish. Fill cavities in apples with mincemeat. Pour apple cider around apples; dot tops of apples with butter. Bake 375° for 30-40 minutes, basting with pan juice several times during cooking. Makes 4 servings.

Bonnie "Gauley" Lovison
Downers Grove

CARRAGEEN MILK PUDDING

Carrageen is an edible form of dry seaweed, rich in vitamins & noted for its gelling properties. It is available in health food or import store.

½ c **tightly packed carrageen (½ oz.)**
boiling water
2 c **milk**
¼ c **sugar**
1 t **vanilla**

Place carrageen in small bowl, add boiling water, stir & drain. Mix this with milk in pan & cook stirring often, over moderate heat, for 15 min. till thick & creamy. Add sugar & vanilla & stir till sugar dissolves. Strain mixture, remove carrageen, & pour into individual molds which have been rinsed in cold water. Refrigerate till set, unmold & serve with whip cream or chocolate sauce. (Lemon pudding: add grated rind of 1 lemon to milk before cooking. Omit vanilla & add ½ t lemon extract; peppermint pudding: omit vanilla, add ¼ t peppermint extract & few drops green food coloring.)

Clare Stephens
Dalkey, Co. Dublin

GOOSEBERRY FOOL

1	#	gooseberries
4		oz. sugar
½		gill water (¼ pint)
¼		pint cream

Top & tail the gooseberries. Wash them & stew with the sugar & water till pulped. Sieve. Whip the cream & combine with the fruit. Serve in small glasses. Other fruits such as strawberries, raspberries, & apricots also make a good fruit fool. The two former should be used without cooking.

Mrs. Newell
28 Kilcoole Park, Belfast

IRISH TRIFLE

Layer bottom of 9x13 glass pan with ½" slices of angel food cake. Spread thin layer of raspberry jam over. Pour sherry over this (amount depends on individual taste). Then layer sliced peaches, vanilla pudding or custard & finally a layer of whipped cream. Can also be made in a glass bowl — attractive & delicious!

Maeve O'Connor
Blackrock, Co. Dublin

OLD BUSHMILLS COFFEE

1   **pint strong hot black coffee**
5   **oz. whipping cream**
Old Bushmills Irish Whiskey
sugar

Warm 4 long-stemmed glasses with boiling water. Place 2 T whiskey & 2 t
sugar in each glass. Pour in coffee & stir. Shake whipping cream carton
by hand till it sounds thickened. Pour cream slowly over back of teaspoon
onto coffee. Try to keep cream from sinking into coffee. Serve immediately.

Caroline Cracroft
British Consulate, Chicago

APPETIZERS
AND
BEVERAGES

Hot Buttered Rum

N. SUFFOLK

TOBY'S RYE ROUNDS

1   #   **lean ground beef**
1   #   **Italian sausage**
1   #   **Velveeta cheese**
½   t   **oregano**
party rye bread

Remove sausage from casing. Cook. Add ground beef and cook till done. Drain. Add cheese and oregano and blend well. Put the meat mixture on rye rounds and it can either be put on cookie sheets and frozen till needed or baked at 350° for 10 min. till hot and bubbly.

Marilyn Hallihan
Arlington Heights

BAMBINI

½ c ricotta cheese
1 c grated mozzarella cheese
¼ c parmesan cheese
1 10 oz. pkg. large flaky refrigerator biscuits
1 3½ oz. pkg. pepperoni

Combine cheeses in small bowl. Halve each biscuit, forming 20 thin biscuits. Shape each biscuit half in 2½" x 4" oval. Place a slice of pepperoni on dough & top with 1 T cheese mixture. Moisten edges & fold dough over to enclose filling, pinch to seal. Place on lightly greased baking sheet and bake at 350° for 20 min. Serve warm.

Marilyn Hallihan
Arlington Heights

COCKTAIL REUBENS

1   pkg. of party rye bread

Top each rye with the following toppings in the following order:

1.   spread each rye with Thousand Island dressing
2.   1 or 2 slices of corned beef
3.   8 oz. can of sauerkraut, drained & snipped, about 1 T on each
4.   6 oz. swiss cheese, put a small slice on each

Bake on a cookie sheet at 400° for 6-8 min. or till cheese melts.

Pat Fortune
Elmhurst

BACON & WATER CHESTNUTS

1   can water chestnuts, cut in half
1   # good quality bacon, cut in thirds

Wrap bacon around chestnuts securing with toothpicks. Bake at 350° for 30 min., on foil lined cookie sheet. At this point you can freeze for later use. When ready to serve drizzle with sauce and reheat at 350° for 20 min.

SAUCE
½   c   catsup
¼   c   white sugar

Linda Wilson
Naperville

ONION BACON APPETIZERS
Simple & Easy!

Amount of ingredients varies according to quantity needed.

Fry bacon in small pieces & drain.
Add chopped green onions.
Add enough mayo to blend other ingredients.
Put a small amount on crackers or rye bread and broil.

Linda Wilson
Naperville

BAKED POTATO SKINS

8		large potatoes, baked & slightly cooled
2	T	melted butter
¾	#	bacon, fried & crumbled
5		fresh green onions, minced
¾	c	grated cheddar cheese

Cut potatoes in half lengthwise, then cut each half into thirds. Scoop out potatoes, leaving skin intact (save potato for later use). Sprinkle skins evenly with butter, then bacon & onions. Top with cheese & bake at 350° for 15 min. or till crisp.

Diane O'Connor
Downers Grove

HOT SPINACH BALLS

2   pkg. frozen chopped spinach, thaw & drain
2   c seasoned stuffing mix
1   c parmesan cheese
¾   c butter melted
5-6   eggs
1   medium onion chopped
garlic powder

Mix all ingredients & roll into 1 inch balls. Bake on cookie sheet for 15-20 min. Can also be frozen (before cooking) on cookie sheet. Store in freezer in plastic bags & then use when needed.

Kathleen Waller
Downers Grove

MAGIC MEATBALLS

1   **12 oz. bottle chili sauce**
¾   c **grape jelly**
2   T **lemon juice**
1   T **salt**
1   # **ground beef, lean**

Combine chili sauce, jelly & lemon juice in 2 qt. saucepan. Shape beef and salt into 1 inch balls. Place in sauce & cook simmering for 30 min. Serve hot with toothpicks.

James & Helen Chevrier
Villa Park

PIZZA SNACKS

¼ c mayo
¼ c chopped black olives
¼ c bacon bits, pepperoni, or cooked sausage
1 T dried chives
1 c grated swiss cheese
party rye

Mix first five ingredients and spread on rye rounds. Place under broiler till bubbly.

Mary Ellen Durbin
Lisle

CRAB AND CREAM CHEESE APPETIZER

8   oz. cream cheese
1   bunch green onions, chopped
1   small jar pimentos
1   6-7 oz. can crabmeat
1   jar cocktail sauce

Soften cream cheese, add onions & drained pimentos. Form cheese into round or rectangle & press drained & rinsed crab on top. Top with cocktail or shrimp sauce. Serve with crackers. Easy and good.

Donna Doherty
Merrillville, Ind.

ELEGANT CRAB

1   pkg. (8 oz.) cream cheese
1   pkg. (6 oz.) frozen crab meat, thawed & drained & chopped (reserve
       2 T liquid)
2   T minced green onion (white part only)
¼   t salt
⅛   t hot pepper sauce
1   t lemon juice
⅓   c sliced almonds

Beat till creamy the cheese, crab liquid (2 T), onion, lemon juice, salt &
pepper. Stir in crab. Turn into greased shallow 3 c baking dish. Sprinkle
with almonds. Bake 350° for 20-30 min. or till bubbly. Serve with bread
rounds or crackers.

Diane House
Deerfield

CRAB APPETIZERS

1   stick margarine
1   jar Old English spread
½   t   mayo
½   t   seasoned salt
7   oz. crab meat
6   English muffins split

Blend the first five ingredients. Spread on each muffin and freeze on cookie sheet. Store in plastic bags in freezer. To serve, cut each muffin into wedges while still frozen. Broil till bubbly.

Jan LeMonnier
Frankfort

BUTTERFLIED BAYOU SHRIMP

1   #   shrimp in shells, uncooked
¼   c   butter or margarine
¼   c   vegetable oil
2   T   lemon juice
¼   t   each salt & pepper
2   T   barbecue sauce
1   bay leaf crumbled
1   garlic clove crushed
½   t   each basil lvs., rosemary lvs., paprika &
         crushed dried red peppers

Butterfly shrimp by cutting lengthwise down back but not all the way thru. Do not remove shells. In large pan melt butter & saute shrimp 3-4 min. or till pink. Add other ingredients & simmer over low heat 3-4 min. Cover & let stand 5 min. Spoon shrimp & sauce into large bowl. Have lots of napkins ready for guests to shell their own shrimp. Makes 35-40 appetizers.

Ginny Hayes
Oak Park

SHRIMP APPETIZER

1 c mayo
1 c shredded cheddar cheese
1   small onion, dice or grate
1   can (6½ oz.) shrimp, drain & crumble

Mix all ingredients, spread on cocktail rye & bake at 400° for 15-20 min. Yields about 24.

Donna T. Bos
Frankfort

ARTICHOKE APPETIZER

2   (14 oz.) cans artichoke hearts, drain & chop
1   c grated parmesan cheese
1   c mayo
1   c slivered almonds

Toast almonds for 10 min. at 350°. Mix all ingredients in 1 qt. dish reserving some almonds to sprinkle on top. Bake at 350° for 20 min. Serve as spread for crackers.

Donna T. Bos
Frankfort

NACHO APPETIZER

1   12 oz. bag round or triangular taco chips
1   can enchilada dip
½ # ground beef
1   pkg. taco seasoning mix
1   8 oz. pkg. cheddar, grated
sour cream and/or guacamole

Cook beef & season mix. Put 1 t enchilada dip on each chip. Top with small amount of meat mix, pressing down lightly. Sprinkle with grated cheese. Bake 350° 8-10 min. or till cheese melts & hot. Serve with sour cream and/or guacamole dip.

Ginny Hayes
Oak Park

CHILI CON QUESO

2   cans chili without beans
1 # cheddar cheese
1   green pepper

Cook 3 hrs. on low in crock pot. Serve with taco or nacho chips.

Lynn Chlada
Cicero

AVOCADO TACO SPREAD

2		ripe avocados, peel & dice
8		oz. cream cheese
½	c	sour cream
2	t	lemon juice
1	t	each garlic & onion salt
4		oz. cheddar cheese shredded

Blend till smooth in blender or mixer. Spread on platter. Cover with fine chopped green onion, lettuce & tomatoes. Top with cheddar cheese & refrigerate till needed. Serve with regular taco or nacho chips.

Linda Wilson
Naperville

PATE DE FOIS GRAS

1 # liverwurst mashed
1   clove garlic pressed
½ t basil
3 T minced onion
1 T dry vermouth

Blend the above & shape into 2 igloos. Chill.

Mix the following ingredients and spread over igloos:

1   8 oz. cream cheese
1   clove garlic pressed
⅛ t tabasco

Then cover with black caviar.

Jackie Brennan
Evanston

TINY CHEESE BITES

1   c   **flour**
1   c   **Rice Krispies**
1   **stick butter**
½   #   **grated sharp cheddar**
¼   t   **salt**
¼   t   **red pepper or to taste**

Blend butter & cheese. Add dry ingredients and mix well. Add cereal & fold in gently. Roll in marble size balls. Put on ungreased cookie sheet. Flatten with thumb. Bake 15-20 minutes in 350° oven.

Rose Bagley
Naperville

HOT CHEESE WONDERS

1   c   grated cheese
½   c   butter
pinch cayenne
1⅛ c   flour

Mix well and make into small balls. Bake 10 minutes at 400°.

Jan LeMonnier
Frankfort

CURRY SPREAD

1		lg. pkg. cream cheese
½	t	curry powder
½	t	salt
1	t	worcestershire sauce
8		dashes tabasco sauce
4		pieces bacon, cooked & crumbled
3	T	toasted chopped pecans

chopped chutney

Mix together the first 5 ingredients, form into a ball & chill. Just before serving top the cheese ball with the chutney, bacon & toasted pecans. Serve with crackers.

Marlene Herrling
Woodbridge, Virginia

CARAWAY DIP

Mix in blender:

8   oz. cream cheese
½ c sour cream
1   stick melted butter
½ t dry mustard
2 t paprika
1 t caraway seed
¼ c chop. green onions

Combine and serve at room temperature with bite size chunks of rye bread.

Beverly Buck
West Dundee

DILL DIP

⅔ c mayonnaise
⅔ c sour cream
1 T onion flakes
1 T parsley flakes
1 t dill weed
1 t bon appetit

Combine and chill. Serve with raw vegetables or cut top off a round loaf and hollow out. Fill with dip and serve with the bread cubes.

Loni Kelly
South Holland

SPINACH DIP

1		pkg. froz. chop. spinach, thaw & drain
1	c	sour cream
1	c	mayonnaise
2		green onions, chopped
1		pkg. Knorr vegetable soup mix
1		can water chestnuts sliced

Combine well and refrigerate. Serve with raw vegetables or bread chunks.

Grace Merrill
Naperville

DEVILED EGG SAIL BOATS

12   **hard cooked eggs**
½ c **mayonnaise**
½ c **pickle relish**
1   T **mustard**

In small bowl mix yolks, mayo, relish, and mustard. Blend well. Fill egg halves. Garnish with a pretzel stick and paper or cheese slice sail.

Sue Hoffman
Westmont

SPICED NUTS

2½ c mixed nuts
Beat till foamy 1 egg white & ½ t water

Stir nuts in egg mixture and then into a combination of ¼ c sugar & 1½ T cinnamon. Place on cookie sheet at 300° for 20-25 minutes. Turn every 5 or 10 minutes because they burn easily.

Linda Wilson
Naperville

BRANDY SLUSH

1		12 oz. can orange juice concentrate
1		12 oz. can lemonade concentrate
4		tea bags
2	c	apricot or peach brandy
9	c	water
1½	c	sugar

Boil 7 c water and dissolve sugar, then cool. Boil 2 c water and steep tea bags for 20 min. Mix all of above together and add lemonade, orange juice and brandy. Freeze, stirring every now and then. Serve scooped in a glass and add 7-Up or ginger ale.

Paula Schumacher
Naperville

FROZEN WHISKEY SOURS

1   **large can frozen lemonade concentrate**
3   **cans water (use empty lemonade cans)**
1½   **cans whiskey**
1   **small can frozen orange juice concentrate**

Put all ingredients in freezer-safe bowl. Cover and freeze. To serve, stir and scoop into cocktail glasses. Makes approximately 12 servings.

Mary Sue Paradiso
Chicago

FIRESIDE COFFEE

2   c   Swiss Miss cocoa
2   c   non-dairy creamer
1   c   instant coffee
1   t   cinnamon
½   t   nutmeg
1½ c   sugar, added last and stirred in

Combine all ingredients except sugar and blend in blender or food processor, 5 min. Stir in sugar. Store in air tight container. Use 2-4 t mix in each cup of boiling water.

Jan LeMonnier
Frankfort

SPICY EGGNOG

½ c sugar
¼ t cinnamon
⅛ t nutmeg
dash allspice
3   eggs, separated
2 c milk
1 c light cream

Combine first 5 ingredients.

Beat at high speed in mixer, egg white till soft peaks form. Slowly beat in ½ of sugar mixture till stiff peaks form.

In small bowl beat yolks till lemon colored. Slowly beat in remaining sugar. Mix till smooth & thick. Thoroughly fold into whites. Stir in milk and cream well. Serve well-chilled, sprinkle with nutmeg. Can also add ½ shot of brandy to each serving if desired.

Jan LeMonnier
Frankfort

HOT COCOA MIX

1	#	Nestles Quick
1		6 oz. coffee creamer
1		box 25 oz. nonfat dry milk
2	c	sugar
½	c	cocoa, optional

Mix all ingredients together, store. When needed use ¼ c mix to 1 c hot water.

Marilyn Ermer
Naperville

HOMEMADE IRISH CREAM

¾ to 1 c good scotch
½   pt. whipping cream
1   can sweetened condensed milk
1   T instant chocolate
a little less than ½ t coconut extract
3   eggs

Blend all ingredients till thick. Refrigerate. I use vinegar bottles at Crate & Barrel to store cream in.

Jackie Brennan
Evanston

SPICED ICED TEA ICE CUBES

2-3   cinnamon sticks
8   whole cloves
2½ c boiling water
4   tea bags
1   6 oz. can frozen lemonade unthawed

Place cinnamon sticks, cloves and tea bags in medium saucepan. Pour boiling water over and simmer over low heat 5 min. Strain tea into bowl. Add lemonade concentrate to tea stirring till melted. Pour tea mixture into ice cube trays. Place a small lemon slice, green maraschino cherry or a mint sprig in each ice cube. Freeze. Place 3-4 ice cubes in glass and add iced tea or lemonade, etc.

Nancy Suffolk
Glendale Heights

BREADS

DELICIOUS FRESH APPLE BREAD

1		stick butter or margarine
2		eggs
¾	c	sugar
2	c	flour
½	t	salt
2	T	sour milk or buttermilk
1	t	each cinnamon & nutmeg
1	t	baking soda
2	c	chopped apples

TOPPING

2	T	sugar
2	T	flour
2	T	melted butter
1	t	cinnamon
½	c	chopped nuts

(To sour milk, add ½ t vinegar to 2 T milk.) Cream butter & sugar, add eggs. Blend in flour & salt & spices. Dissolve 1 t soda in milk & add to batter. Fold in chopped apples (I leave skins on). Mix topping & sprinkle over. Makes two 7x3 breads or 1 doz. muffins. Grease pans & bake at 350° for 40-50 min., muffins for 25-30 min.

Mary Wilson
Wheaton

PUMPKIN BREAD

⅔ c Crisco
2⅔ c sugar
4   eggs
2   c pumpkin
⅔ c water
3⅓ c flour
2   t baking soda
1½ t salt
½ t baking powder
1   t cinnamon
1   t cloves
⅔ c nuts
⅔ c raisins

Grease two 9x5 loaf pans or three 7x3. In large bowl cream crisco & sugar till fluffy. Stir in eggs, pumpkin & water. Blend all dry ingred. into above, stir in nuts & raisins. Pour in pans. Bake 50-60 min. at 350° or till toothpick comes out clean.

Mary Beth Butler
Oak Park

ZUCCHINI PINEAPPLE BREAD

3   eggs
1   c   oil
2   c   sugar
2   t   vanilla
2   c   shredded unpeeled zucchini
1   8¼ oz. can crushed pineapple, drain well
3   c   flour
2   t   baking soda
1½ t   cinnamon
1   t   salt
¾   t   nutmeg
¼   t   baking powder
1   c   each chopped dates *or* raisins & chopped nuts

Beat eggs, oil, sugar, & vanilla till thick. Stir in remaining ingred. Mix well. Pour into 2 greased 9x5 loaf pans. Bake 350° about 1 hour or till toothpick comes out clean.

Linda Neal
Valparaiso, Ind.

GRAPENUT BREAD

1	c	Grapenuts cereal
2	c	buttermilk
1	c	sugar
3		egg yolks
½	t	salt
3½	c	flour
1	t	baking soda
2		heaping t baking powder
3		egg whites

Soak Grapenuts in buttermilk 5-10 min. Add sugar, yolks, & salt, mix well. Sift dry ingredients & add to creamed mixture. Beat egg whites stiff & fold into batter. Pour into greased loaf pans (2). Bake at 350° for 1 hour.

Jane O'Hare
Downers Grove

CARROT-PINEAPPLE BREAD

3	c	flour
2	c	sugar
1	t	salt
½	t	cinnamon
½	t	nutmeg
½	t	baking soda
1	c	oil
3		eggs
1		8 oz. can crushed pineapple
2	c	grated carrots

Sift all dry ingredients. Add 1 c salad oil & mix well. Beat in eggs one at a time, mixing well after each. Stir in pineapple & juice & grated carrots. Bake in greased loaf pans: two 9x5's or three 7x3's. temp. 350° for 45 min. or till toothpick comes out clean.

Mary Wilson
Wheaton

"FIVE STAR" SUPREME BLUEBERRY MUFFINS

¼	c	butter or margarine
½	c	sugar
1		egg
¾	c	milk
¼	t	vanilla
1¾	c	flour
2½	t	baking powder
½	t	salt
1	c	blueberries

Cream butter & sugar till light. Beat in egg, then milk & vanilla. Beat in dry ingredients just till moistened. Fold in blueberries. Spoon into muffin liners, makes 1 dz. Bake at 425° for 20-25 min. To enrich the muffins I add 2-3 T wheat germ or Cornell Triple Rich Formula (for each cup of flour add 1 T soy flour, 1 T dry milk, 1 t wheat germ). This will enrich the flour to almost as much as whole wheat. DELICIOUS MUFFINS WHETHER JUST OUT OF THE OVEN OR COLD THE NEXT DAY!

Diane O'Connor
Downers Grove

RAISIN BRAN MUFFIN MIX

1		15 oz. box Raisin Bran Flakes
3	c	sugar
5	c	flour
5	t	soda
2	t	salt

Mix all ingredients. Make well in middle and add:

4		beaten eggs
1	c	vegetable oil
1		qt. buttermilk

Mix well & keep in refrigerator. Keeps up to 6 weeks. When ready to serve, fill muffin cup ⅔ full and bake 400° for 15-18 min.

Sharon Zieman
Downers Grove

APPLE STREUSEL COFFEE CAKE

STREUSEL

½ c packed brown sugar

1 t cinnamon

2 T butter

½ c chopped nuts

COFFEE CAKE

2 c unbleached flour

⅔ c sugar

⅓ c wheat germ

8 oz. plain or vanilla yogurt

½ c butter

1 c fine. chop. apples

2 eggs

½ t salt

1 t vanilla

1 t each baking powder & soda

In small bowl combine all streusel ingredients. In mixer combine all coffee cake ingredients except apples. Beat at low speed till moistened & med. speed till well mixed. Spread ½ of batter into greased & floured 10" bundt or tube pan. Layer with ½ streusel, apples & then remaining batter. Top with rest of streusel. Bake at 350° for 40-50 min. or till toothpick comes out clean. Cool in pan on rack 15 min. & then invert onto rack to finish cooling. Can glaze with a thin powdered sugar frosting.

Diane O'Connor
Downers Grove

NO KNEAD COFFEECAKE

4	c	flour
1	t	sugar
1	c	shortening (½ butter & ½ margarine)
1	c	milk
1		pkg. dry yeast
3		beaten egg yolks, reserve whites at room temperature

Sift flour, salt, sugar. Cut in shortening as in pie. In small bowl blend milk, yeast, eggs. Stir in above ingred. & mix well. Cover with plastic wrap & light towel & refrigerate overnight. Divide in 2-3 parts. Roll out ½" thick and add filling. Sprinkle chopped nuts & cinnamon over filling. Roll & put in pan to rise for 1 hour. Bake 40 min. 350° oven or till lightly browned. Frost with thin icing while warm & top with nuts.

Filling: Beat 3 egg whites from above, till stiff, then beat in 1 c sugar till stiff.

Mary Grace Butler
Oak Park

SWEDISH COFFEECAKE

BOTTOM LAYER

1   c   flour
½   c   butter
2   T   water

Cut butter into flour till crumbly. Sprinkle with water, mix with fork and divide dough in half. Pat into 2 strips, 12″ by 3″ apart on ungreased baking sheet.

TOP LAYER

½   c   butter
1   c   water
1   t   almond flavoring
1   c   flour
3   eggs

Mix butter and water and bring to boil. Remove from heat, add almond & beat in flour fast to prevent lumping. Add eggs one at a time, beating well till smooth. Divide in ½ and spread on each strip of pastry. Bake 45 min. at 350°. (Top layer will puff while baking and then shrink while cooling leaving a custardy center. Can frost with a powdered sugar frosting & top with shredded almonds if desired.)

Mary Ellen Durbin
Lisle

CINNAMON NUT KUCHEN

½ c butter or margarine
¾ c sugar
1 t vanilla
3   eggs
2 c flour
1 t baking powder
1 t baking soda
½   pint sour cream

Cream butter, sugar & vanilla. Add eggs, beat well. Sift flour, powder & soda and add to creamed mixture alternately with sour cream. Spread ½ batter into greased 10 inch tube pan. Sprinkle ½ of nut mixture (6 T butter, 1 c brown sugar packed, 2 T cinnamon, 1 c chopped nuts) over batter and then fill with remaining batter. Sprinkle last of nut mixture on top. Bake at 350° for 40-45 min.

Marie Lee
Frankfort

OVEN APPLE PANCAKES

4		eggs, beaten
1	c	each: milk, unbleached flour
¼	t	salt
½	c	sugar
1	T	cinnamon
3		apples, cored & cut into ¼" wedges
¼	c	butter

Combine eggs, milk, flour & salt, beat with whisk or rotary beater till smooth. Mix sugar & cinnamon & toss with apples to coat. Grease two 9" pie plates with butter. Put ½ of apples in each plate. Pour ½ of batter over apples in each plate. Bake at 375° for 30-35 min. or till light brown. Serve hot, cut into wedges.

Donna Doherty
Merrillville, Ind.

PARMESAN GARLIC BUBBLE LOAF

1	#	frozen bread dough, thawed
3	T	grated parmesan cheese
1		garlic clove, minced
¼	c	butter melted

Cut dough into 16 pieces. Shape in balls. Place on floured surface. Cover & let rest 10 min. Stir parmesan & garlic into butter. Using a spoon, roll balls in butter mixture. Arrange the balls loosely in 2 layers in a greased 8″ cake pan or 9x5 loaf pan. Let rise in a warm place till doubled. Bake in 375° oven for 20 min. or till golden brown. This bread freezes well. Thaw & reheat at 350°.

Marilyn Hallihan
Arlington Heights

MONKEY BREAD

2   pkg. refrigerator biscuits, cut into 4 pieces each

Shake biscuit pieces in mixture of ½ c brown sugar & 1 t cinnamon.

Drop into loaf pan.

Mix in another pan & bring to boil:

1   stick margarine
¼ c brown sugar
¼ c white sugar

Pour over biscuits & bake for 30-35 min.

Beverly Buck
Dundee

"NO FAIL" WHOLE WHEAT-OATMEAL BREAD

2	c	oatmeal	2	c	cold water
¾	c	oil	3		pkg. yeast, dissolved in
¼	c	brn. sugar			½ cup warm water
¼	c	molasses	½	c	wheat germ
1	T	salt	4	c	whole wheat flour
2	c	boiling water	6-7	c	unbleached flour

Mix first 5 ingredients in very large bowl. Add the boiling water & stir well, add the cold water & stir well again. Add the dissolved yeast & mix well. Add wheat germ & the flours till it becomes difficult to mix. Turn out on floured surface & knead in remaining flour, add more flour than called for if still sticky. Knead till smooth. Place dough in greased bowl & let rise till doubled. Turn out & knead down & divide into loaves 6 (7x3), 5 (9x5). Place formed loaves into greased pans & cover to let rise till doubled. Bake at 375° about 30 min. or till they sound hollow when tapped on bottom. Then turn out on racks to cool (can substitute ½ c honey for brown sugar & molasses).

Diane O'Connor
Downers Grove

HONEY EGG BREAD

2   pkg. dry yeast
2¼ c warm water
½   c honey
1   T salt
¼   c oil
2   eggs room temp.
6 or 7 c flour

Dissolve yeast in warm water in large bowl. Add honey, salt, oil & eggs, mix well. Stir in flour one cup at a time till dough will accept no more flour. Knead about 7 min. Cover with plastic wrap & then a light cloth. Let rise till double in bulk. Punch down & shape in 2 loaves and place in greased pans. Cover & let rise again (30-45) minutes. Bake at 400° for 30 min. or till bread is brown. For a soft crust brush with butter while loaves are hot. Crisp crust, let cool without butter.

Mary Grace Butler
Oak Park

"IRISH COFFEE" CAKE

1		pkg. Pillsbury Bundt Pound Cake Supreme
3		eggs
1	c	water
½	c	whiskey
¼	c	margarine or butter
2	T	brown sugar
1	T	instant coffee

Grease & flour 12 c bundt pan. In large bowl, blend packets 1 and 2 and remaining ingredients till moistened, beating 2 min. at medium speed. Pour in prepared pan. Bake 325° for 45-55 min. or till toothpick comes out clean. Cool till lukewarm & invert on serving plate. Sprinkle topping packet over cool cake. Serve as is or with whipped cream.

Mary Grace Butler
Oak Park

SOUPS AND SALADS

HEARTY HAM & BEAN SOUP

½ # navy beans washed well, covered with 6 c warm water & let stand overnight. Next day pour beans & water they were soaking in, into a large pan.

Ham bone & any small bits of ham
1   onion chopped & sauteed
¾ c shredded raw potatoes
¾ c chopped celery
¼ c chopped celery leaves
¼ t pepper
½ c drained tomatoes cut in pieces
½ c fresh green onion tops
about 2 t salt

Combine all except tomatoes & green onion tops & cook in covered pan slowly about 3 hrs. or till beans are very soft. If too thin, cook uncovered a little while. If too thick add a little water or stock. Add tomatoes & onion tops the last 10 min. & cook uncovered.

Marilyn Hallihan
Arlington Heights

CLEAR MUSHROOM SOUP

3	T	olive oil
1		medium onion, sliced
3½	c	water
1		clove garlic sliced
½	#	mushrooms sliced
½	t	sage
½	t	rosemary
½	t	oregano
1	t	salt

nutmeg
fresh ground black pepper
lemon juice

Heat oil in skillet. Saute onions slowly till lightly browned. Pour in water, garlic, mushrooms, herbs, salt, nutmeg & pepper to taste. Add a little lemon juice if you want.

Denise Bell
Schaumburg

BEST ONION SOUP

4 T butter
2 T oil
2 # onions, thinly sliced (7 c)
1 t salt
3 T flour
2   qt. beef stock (1 qt. beef & 1 qt. chicken)

Melt butter & oil, stir in onion & salt. Cook slowly (20-30) min. till onions are golden. Sprinkle flour, stir 2-3 min. Heat stock in separate pan till it simmers. Pour over onions & stir. Simmer partially covered 30-40 min. Add 1 c sherry. Serve with french bread.

Jill Brown
Wilmette

ARTICHOKE SOUP SUPREME

1		can 12 oz. artichoke hearts
1		can 13¾ oz. chicken broth
1	t	lemon juice
4	t	minced green onion, sauteed in butter

pinch nutmeg

pepper to taste

| 1 | c | (½ pt.) whipping cream |
| 5-6 | | thin lemon slices |

Rinse & drain artichokes. Put in blender or processor with broth. Blend 1 min. Pour into saucepan with lemon juice, onion, nutmeg & pepper. Bring to boil. Remove from heat & add cream. Heat on low, do not boil. Float lemon slice on each serving for garnish.

Ginny Hayes
Oak Park

CHEESE SOUP DELIGHT

2   T   margarine or butter
3   T   flour
1   c   milk
1   can chicken broth
3   T   white wine or beer
¼   t   worcestershire sauce
dash hot pepper sauce
⅛   t   salt
1   c   shredded sharp cheddar

In pan over medium heat, melt margarine, stir in flour. Heat till bubbly stirring constantly. Gradually add milk & chicken broth, stir till smooth and thickened. Add wine, worcestershire sauce, hot pepper sauce & salt. Simmer 3-4 min. Add cheese, remove from heat & stir till melted & mixture smooth.

Jan LeMonnier
Frankfort

CHEESE CHOWDER

2 c diced potatoes
½ c sliced carrots
½ c sliced celery
¼ c chopped onion
1½ t salt
¼ t pepper
2 c boiling water
¼ c margarine
¼ c flour
2 c milk
10 oz. shredded cheddar
2 cans cream corn

Combine first 7 ingredients, cover & simmer 10 min. Do not drain. Make a sauce with margarine, flour & milk. Add cheese, stir till melted. Add corn & vegetables. Heat, do not boil.

MaryAnn O'Brien
Frankfort

FULL-BODIED & SAVORY MINESTRONE SOUP

3		slices bacon, finely chopped
1	c	chopped onion
½	c	chopped celery
2		lg. cloves garlic minced
1	t	basil, crushed
1		can beef broth
1		can bean with bacon soup
1½		soup cans water
1		can 16 oz. tomatoes
½	c	uncooked elbow macaroni
1	c	cabbage cut in long shreds
½	t	salt
1	c	cubed zucchini

In large pan brown bacon & cook onion, celery, garlic & basil till tender. Stir in soups, water, tomatoes, macaroni & salt. Bring to boil, cover, reduce heat & simmer 15 min. Add cabbage and zucchini and cook 10 min. or till done.

Judy Oslack
Downers Grove

CARROT-ORANGE SOUP

1   # carrots
2   pt. chicken broth
½ c orange juice
1   bunch shallots chopped

Simmer all ingredients till soft. Put in blender or food processor and puree. Delicious served hot or cold.

Mrs. Gordon Jewkes
Wife of British Consul-General, Chicago

OYSTER STEW

1   12 oz. can oysters undrained
2   c half & half
2   T margarine
¼ t black pepper
¼ t paprika
¼ t salt
dash of celery salt

Heat oysters in liquid until edges curl. Add half & half, margarine, paprika, salt & celery salt. Heat gently just till mixture is hot. Don't boil or overcook.

Linda Dalton
Joliet

MARINATED VEGETABLE SALAD

⅔ c oil
⅔ c cider vinegar
2 t oregano
1 t basil
1 t marjoram
1 t salt
1 t sugar
¼ c chop. onion
¼ c chop. parsley
1 T lemon juice

Mix dressing and pour over following vegetables:

1   pt. cherry tomatoes
1 # cauliflower
1 # broccoli
¾ # mushrooms
1 # sliced zucchini
1   bag carrots sliced thin

Marinate all vegetables, except mushrooms, overnight. Add mushrooms before ready to serve. Drain marinade & save for dressing.

Patti Peckhart
Downers Grove

TOSSED MANDARIN SALAD

1   bunch romaine
½   head lettuce
1   bunch green onions sliced
2   stalks celery chopped
1   can mandarin oranges, drained
½   c   candied almonds

DRESSING
½   t   salt
pepper to taste
2   T   sugar
2   T   white vinegar
¼   c   olive oil
2   T   chopped parsley

Candied Almonds: Place ½ c sliced almonds & 3 T sugar in fry pan. Stir over low heat till sugar melts and almonds are coated. Cool & break apart.

Mix salad ingredients, toss with dressing. Sprinkle with mandarin oranges & then almonds.

Bonnie Dee
Troy, Ohio

RICH 'N CHARLIES SALAD

romaine & iceberg lettuce
small jar pimento drained
1   16 oz. can artichoke hearts, drained & cut
salt & pepper to taste
parmesan cheese to taste
sliced red onions

Wash & separate lettuce into bite size pieces. Add the rest of the ingredients. When ready toss with dressing.

DRESSING
¾   c   **olive oil**
¼   c   **vinegar**
¼   c   **parmesan cheese**

SPINACH SALAD WITH BEAN SPROUTS

1   bag spinach, rinse & dry
1 c fresh bean sprouts or 1 can
1   can water chestnuts, drained & sliced
8   strips bacon, cooked & crumbled
4   hard cooked eggs, sliced

DRESSING — combine in blender:
1 c oil
¾ c sugar
¼ c vinegar
½ t salt
⅓ c ketchup
2 T worcestershire sauce
dash onion salt

Toss salad with dressing just before serving.

Paula Schumacher
Naperville

WILTED SPINACH SALAD

6		slices diced bacon
1	t	sugar
¼	c	white wine vinegar
¼	t	salt
¼	t	dry mustard
½	c	sour cream
6	c	washed & dried spinach leaves
3		green onions, thinly sliced

Cook bacon till crisp, drain all but 2 T fat from drippings. Whisk vinegar, sugar, salt, mustard & pepper into skillet, cook till heated through. Remove from heat & stir in sour cream. DO NOT BOIL.

Put spinach & onions in serving bowl, toss with warm dressing. Sprinkle with cooked bacon. Serve immediately.

Jill Brown
Wilmette

SPINACH-BACON SALAD BOWL

¾ c French dressing as follows:

¾ t salt
sp̔ ck of pepper
dash paprika
¼ t sugar
¼ c lemon juice or vinegar
¾ c salad oil
6   cloves garlic, chopped
½ t caraway seeds, optional

Combine French dressing ingredients & let sit for several hours. Layer 1#
of spinach, 8 bacon slices, cooked, fresh mushrooms & 3 sliced hard
cooked eggs. Right before serving toss with dressing.

Sheila McCann
Lisle

SEVEN LAYER SALAD

1   head lettuce
⅓   c   green onion finely chopped
⅓   c   celery sliced
1   can water chestnuts
1   10 oz. pkg. frozen peas
1   #   bacon fried, drained & crumbled

Layer all of the above. Put 2 c mayo on top & seal all the way around.
Sprinkle 2 T sugar over mayo. Sprinkle parmesan or romano cheese on
top of that. Cover & leave in refrigerator overnight. When ready to serve
slice hard cooked eggs & tomatoes on top.

Sharon Urba
Mokena

CHINESE CHICKEN SALAD

3   whole chicken breasts—poached & shredded
1   lg. head lettuce, shredded
3-4   green onions chopped
1   pkg. slivered almonds, toasted
1   can sliced water chestnuts
1   (5 oz.) can chow mein noodles (I prefer the rice noodles)

DRESSING
4 T sugar
2½ t salt
1 t Accent
¼ t white pepper
4 T rice vinegar
¼ c salad oil
¼ c sesame oil

Combine salad ingredients & add dressing just before serving.

Donna T. Bos
Frankfort

ARTICHOKE & RICE SALAD

1		pkg. chicken Rice-a-Roni
1		(6 oz.) jar marinated artichokes
4		green onions, sliced thin
½		green pepper, chopped
12		green olives, sliced
½	c	thin sliced celery
1	c	diced shrimp, ham or chicken

DRESSING

½	c	mayo
½	c	sour cream
¾	t	curry powder

reserved artichoke marinade

Cook rice according to directions, omitting butter. Cool. Drain artichokes & save marinade. Cut artichokes in half, add to rice and add remaining ingredients. Toss rice mixture with dressing & chill.

Cindy Fischer
Frankfort

STEAK SALAD

1   #   Sirloin steak — cut into cubes
¼   c   mayonnaise
¼   c   sour cream
1   T   sweet relish
1   T   lemon juice
pinch sugar
1   T   Dijon mustard

Brown steak in butter or oil — remove from heat. While meat is browning mix all other ingredients and gently fold in meat. Serve warm on a bed of lettuce, garnish with quartered egg, tomato and lemon wedges.

Bonnie Lovison
Downers Grove

TACO SALAD

1		pkg. taco seasoning mix
1	#	ground beef
2		tomatoes
1		red onion
1		can ranch-style beans
1		head lettuce
2		avocados
1	c	grated cheddar
1		sm. pkg. taco doritos, crushed
1		bottle garlic french dressing

Brown meat, prepare with taco seasoning according to directions. Cool.
Chop vegetables, add beans, cheese & chips. Add dressing just before
serving. Mix well.

Donna Farrell
Naperville

HOT BAKED POTATO SALAD

8		medium potatoes, pared & cut into ⅛'s
2		8 oz. pkg. American cheese
⅓	c	chopped scallions
⅓	c	chopped green pepper
1	c	mayo
¾	c	sour cream
½	T	salt
⅛	t	pepper
½	c	chopped uncooked bacon (about 5-7 slices)
½	c	sliced pitted ripe olives (about 12)

In lightly greased 3 qt. casserole, combine potatoes, cheese, scallions, green peppers, mayo, sour cream, & seasonings. Stir until well mixed. Sprinkle with bacon & olives. Bake at 350° for 1 hour.

Jan LeMonnier
Frankfort

ORANGE TAPIOCA SALAD

1   3 oz. box orange Jello
1   3 oz. box vanilla pudding mix
1   3 oz. box orange tapioca
1   can mandarin oranges
1 # can crushed pineapple

Drain juice of fruits & add enough water to make 2¾ c. Add to powders & cook till thickened, over low heat. Add oranges & pineapple. Chill. Fold in medium container cool whip or whipped cream.

Mildred King
Iowa

APRICOT JELLO SALAD

1   c   boiling water
2   small pkgs. gelatin
1   c   cold water
1   small sour cream
1   medium can pineapple (crushed)

Mix the boiling water & gelatin & dissolve. Add the cold water. Refrigerate & when it starts to jell add the sour cream & drained pineapple. Add sliced bananas if you like.

Colleen Murphy
Oaklawn

HAWAIIAN FANTASY SALAD

1	#	carton sour cream
3	c	miniature marshmallows
1	#	can pineapple chunks
1		small can mandarin oranges
1		can flaked coconut
1		small jar cherries
1	c	walnut chunks

Drain cherries, pineapple, & oranges. Cut cherries in half. Place all ingredients in large bowl & mix well. Chill 4 hrs. or overnight.

Denise Bell
Schaumburg

FRESH FRUIT SALAD

½   cantaloupe
2   apples
2   oranges peeled
1   pt. strawberries
2   bananas
2   slices watermelon

DRESSING
1   T lemon juice
½   c water
¼   c sugar or ¼ c honey

Peel fruit & slice into ½ inch sections. Combine in bowl. Add the dressing & mix gently. Cover & refrigerate till time to serve. May be topped with strawberry cream:

1   pt. whipping cream, whipped
½   pt. strawberries, mashed

Stir the above two together.

Mary Grace Butler
Oak Park

ENTREES

N.SUFFOLK

DENNIS DAY'S STEAK SAUCE

2 cloves garlic, crushed
½ c soy sauce
¼ c brown sugar
2 T olive oil
¼ t cracked pepper
2 small pieces ginger root or grated fresh ginger

Combine all ingredients in jar or bottle. Cover and shake well before using. Marinate steak one hour in mixture, baste frequently with sauce while broiling.

Dennis Day
California

TERYAKI FLANK STEAK

¼ c white wine (sherry or dry sauterne)
½ c water
2 t sugar
½-1t dry ginger
½   bottle (5 oz.) soy sauce
2   cloves garlic, diced

The above will cover 2 flank steaks. Score steaks & marinate for 6 hours or more. Grill on the outside barbecue until done to your liking.

Judy Pease
Hinsdale

SAUCY STEAK

Brown 2 # chuck or round steak in preheated 425° oven for 20 min. Drain. Reduce temperature to 325° & combine ½ c water, ¼ c catsup, 2 T brown sugar, 2 T worcestershire sauce & 1 t salt. Pour over meat, cover tightly & bake till tender about 1½ hours. Can be made ahead & refrigerated till needed.

Vonnie Philgreen
Downers Grove

BAR-BA-QUED ROAST BEEF

4 # chuck roast, cooked very tender. Cool & cut meat off, discarding fat.

Bring following ingredients to a boil & stir 15 min.:

1		can beer
½	t	salt
1	c	catsup
⅓	c	vinegar
⅓	c	brown sugar
3	T	worcestershire sauce
1	t	dry mustard
1	t	paprika
½	t	chili powder

Add 1 medium onion & juice of ½ lemon, cook 30 min. Add meat & stir, add 1 T honey & mix well. Serve.

Paula Schumacher
Naperville

ORIENTAL BEEF RIBS

10 # beef short ribs
4-5 green onions
2 T toasted sesame seeds
3-4 garlic cloves
1½ c soy sauce
½ c water
1 T Accent
1 T pepper
1½ T sesame oil
2-3 T sugar

Chop onions & garlic, add to other ingredients, mix well & place in large pan or bowl. Let stand overnight in refrigerator, turning meat occasionally. With knife, loosen meat from bone & score larger pieces. Cook over charcoal fire till desired doneness is reached.

Jack Kielczynski
La Grange

ZESTY SHORT RIBS OF BEEF

4	#	meaty beef short ribs
1		lg. tomato chopped
1	c	beef bouillon
¼	c	burgundy wine
¼	c	chopped onion
2	T	horseradish
¼	t	ground ginger
2	T	cornstarch

Brown short ribs & drain fat. In roaster, slow cooker or electric frypan combine meat & other ingredients except cornstarch. Cover & cook:

oven: 350° for 1½-2hr.
crockpot: low, 6-8 hr.
electric frypan: simmer 2½-3 hr.

Remove meat when cooked, dissolve cornstarch in small amount of water & stir into meat juices. Cook & stir till gravy thickens, serve over meat.

Ginny Hayes
Oak Park

FRENCH OVEN BEEF STEW

2	#	cubed beef
2		medium onions, chopped
3		stalks celery, cut in 1" pieces
4		medium carrots, cut in chunks
1	c	tomato juice
⅓	c	quick cooking tapioca
1	T	sugar
1	T	salt
½	t	basil
¼	t	pepper
2		potatoes, cut into quarters

Combine beef, onions, celery, carrots, tomato juice, tapioca, sugar, salt & pepper, & basil in 2½ qt. casserole. Cover & cook in 300° oven for 2½ hr. Put in potatoes & cook for one more hour.

Mildred King (Bonnie's aunt)
Iowa

FUN STEW

2	#	beef cubes
2	T	flour
salt & pepper		
4		potatoes, quartered
4		carrots
1		can green beans
1		can corn
1		can tomato soup
1		cup wine

Flour meat cubes. Place all ingredients in pan with tight fitting lid. Cover tightly, may use foil underneath lid to make very tight seal. Place in oven at 250° for 5 hours. NO PEEKING! Serve over bed of rice.

Jan LeMonnier
Frankfort

CASSEROLE PEPPER STEAK

1½-2 # round steak
1   pkg. dry onion soup mix
1   can Hunts tomato sauce
1   can mushroom soup
1   green pepper sliced thin
1   t soy sauce

Slice steak into thin strips. Put tomato sauce in casserole first, then sliced steak, sprinkle onion soup over, sliced peppers on top of all. Finally top with mushroom soup & soy sauce. Cover tightly & bake at 325° for 1½ hours, take lid off & stir well. Cover again & bake another 30-45 min. or till done. Serve over rice or cooked noodles.

Donna Doherty
Merrillville, Ind.

RANCH ROUND STEAK

3   #   round steak, ½" thick, cut in serving sizes
¼   c   all purpose flour
2   t   dry mustard
¼   c   salad oil
1   T   worcestershire sauce

Combine flour, mustard, 1½ t salt & ⅛ pepper & coat meat, reserving flour mixture. Brown meat on both sides in hot oil. Push meat to side, & stir in reserved flour mix. Combine ½ c water & worcestershire sauce & stir into skillet. Cook till thickened. Reduce heat & simmer covered for 1-1¼ hours till tender. Serves 8.

Jan LeMonnier
Frankfort

SUPER BRISKET

Cover brisket with liquid smoke, garlic powder, salt & celery salt. Cover with foil. Allow to stand overnight in refrigerator. Sprinkle with pepper & worcestershire sauce. Bake at 275° for 5 hours leaving covered. Drain grease and pour the following sauce over. Mix & boil 15 min.:

1	c	catsup
1	t	salt
¼	c	brown sugar
¼	c	worcestershire
2	c	water
1		chopped onion
¼	c	vinegar

Marilyn Ermer
Naperville

CHOP SUEY

1½ # chop suey meat
1   onion, chopped
1   c celery, chopped
salt & pepper to taste
½ T bead molasses
1   can bean sprouts
½ c soy sauce
3 T cornstarch
1 c water

Brown meat, saute onion, celery till tender. Add salt & pepper. Mix soy sauce & cornstarch together & add to meat mixture. Add molasses & water & cook on low heat for about 2 hours. Mix in drained bean sprouts & heat through. Serve over rice. Serves 6

Karon Hunt
Chicago Heights

PORK CHOPS & POTATOES IN CASSEROLE

4   pork chops, 1″ thick
1   # potatoes, raw & sliced
¼   c butter
½   # onions sliced thin
1½ c crushed tomatoes & juice
2   T flour
½   t salt
¼   t pepper
¼   marjoram

Brown pork chops in butter, season with salt & pepper. In a baking dish place ½ of sliced potatoes, then onions, salt & pepper, then rest of potatoes. Place chops next. Add flour to drippings in pan & mix till smooth, slowly add tomatoes & juice. Add marjoram. Cook sauce till thick & pour over meat. Cover with foil & bake at 350° for 1 hr., less time if chops are thin. Check meat & potatoes after 50 min.

Marilyn Hallihan
Arlington Heights

VITELLO ALLA VERONA

8   veal cutlets, 1/8" thick
flour, salt & pepper, olive oil
1½ T butter & flour
1½ c milk
⅓ c dry white wine
pinch of basil
1   c mayo
1   c parmesan cheese
14   oz. artichoke hearts, drain & chop.
2   garlic cloves, chop.

Dust cutlets with flour, salt & pepper. Lightly brown on both sides in olive oil. Take meat out & add flour, butter, & ¼ t salt & basil to pan. Slowly add milk & wine & simmer till thickened. In another bowl mix mayo, parmesan ch., artichokes & garlic, salt & pepper. Spoon equal amounts of mixture onto each cutlet, roll up & place seam down in casserole dish. Pour sauce over. Melt 4 T butter & mix ½ c fresh bread crumbs in, sprinkle over casserole. Bake at 350° for 45-60 min.

Paula Schumacher
Naperville

HAM & BROCCOLI CASSEROLE

1		11 oz. pkg. frozen broccoli	¼	t	pepper
1	c	diced ham	½	t	steak sauce
1	c	diced cooked potatoes	2	t	prepared mustard
⅓	c	butter	¼	c	grated cheese
¼	c	flour	½	t	salt
2	c	milk			

Cook broccoli just till tender. Mix with ham & potatoes in shallow 2 qt. baking dish. Melt butter & blend in ¼ c flour, slowly add 2 c milk, stir till thick. Add pepper, steak sauce, mustard, cheese & salt, stir till cheese melts. Pour over ham & broccoli. Mix the following topping & drop by T onto mixture. Bake at 425° for 25-30 min.:

1	c	flour	2	T	chop. parsley
1½	t	baking powder	2½	T	oil
½	t	salt	⅓	c	milk

Rose Bagley
Naperville

SHRIMP DELIGHT

1   **can shrimp soup**
1   **small can tuna**
½ c **shredded cheddar cheese**
¼ c **milk**
1   **small jar mushrooms**

Saute mushrooms in 2 T butter. Add the remaining ingredients & heat till cheese melts. Serve over rice.

Robin Biesen
New Lenox

JAMBALAYA

1   8 oz. pkg. brn. & serve sausage links
2 c uncooked minute rice
2 c water
1   16 oz. can stewed tomatoes
1   12 oz. pkg. frozen shrimp
2 T instant minced onion
2 t instant chicken bouillon
1 t salt
¼ t each thyme & chili powder
⅛ t cayenne
½ c chopped green pepper

Cut sausages into 1″ pieces & brown. Add remaining ingredients except peppers. Heat stirring occasionally, to boiling, reduce heat. Simmer uncovered 10 min., stir in green pepper.

Linda Dalton
Joliet

MARINATED SHRIMP

2-2½ # shrimp, fresh or frozen
seafood seasoning
4   med. onions sliced thin
box of bay leaves

Cook shrimp in seafood seasoning, rinse & cool. Use glass pan or bowl. Arrange layers of shrimp, onions & bay leaves.

Combine:

1½ c   salad oil
¾   c   warmed white vinegar
1½ t   salt
2½ t   celery seed
2½ T   capers & juice
few drops hot sauce
1   T   yellow mustard

Pour sauce over shrimp, onions & bay leaves. Cover pan & refrigerate for 24 hours. Keeps for 2 weeks, stir once a day.

Jill Brown
Wilmette

SHRIMP CREOLE

1	c	uncooked rice
3		onions, sliced
1		bunch celery, chop.
4	T	bacon fat
2	T	flour
⅛	t	pepper
2	t	chili powder
2	c	water
3	c	can tomatoes
3	c	drained peas
1½	T	vinegar
2	t	sugar
3	c	cooked shrimp

Cook rice & set aside. Brown onion & celery in bacon fat. Blend flour & other seasonings & add water slowly, stirring constantly. Simmer for 15 min. covered. Add remaining ingredients & continue cooking for 10-15 min. or till shrimp heated. Mix in rice & serve.

Patricia Richardson
Chicago

ROQUEFORT & SHRIMP STUFFED SOLE

1	c	butter, soft
4		oz. cream cheese
6		oz. raw shrimp, cut in pcs.
6		oz. Roquefort cheese
2	T	lemon juice
2	t	Pernod or anisette (opt.)
1	t	ea. chop. parsley & chives
1		green onion, minced
⅛	t	hot pepper sauce
⅛	t	worcestershire sauce

salt & pepper to taste

8		(10 oz.) fillets of sole (if 10 oz. fillets not available, use several 5-6 oz. fillets & overlap them when rolling to make a thicker fillet)
2		beaten eggs

breadcrumbs

½	c	melted butter

sauteed mushrooms (opt.)

Combine first 11 ingredients in bowl & blend well. Refrigerate at least 20 min. Pat fish dry. Spread about ¼ c chilled filling on darker side of each fillet. Roll fillets about halfway, carefully fold in outer edges to hold mixture inside, complete rolling. Dip each fillet in beaten eggs & then roll in crumbs. Place in shallow, buttered baking dish just large enough to hold fillets. (If preferred, place rolled fillets in dish without egg & breadcrumbs.) Top with remaining filling, if any & drizzle with melted butter. Bake at 375° for 20 min. or till sole is white & flaky, but not dry. Do Not Overcook! Check often after 15 min. Top with sauteed mushrooms just before serving, if desired.

Judy Pease
Hinsdale

TUNA PUFF SANDWICHES

7		oz. can tuna
1½	t	mustard
¼	t	worcestershire sauce
¼	c	mayo
1½	t	grated onion
2	T	chopped green pepper
3		hamburger buns
¼	c	chopped American cheese
½	c	mayo
6		slices tomato

Blend first 6 ingredients & pile on bun halves. Top each with a tomato slice. Blend ½ c mayo and cheese & spread on tomato. Broil 4" from flame till topping puffs & browns.

Mary Grace Butler
Oak Park

24 HOUR WINE & CHEESE STRATA

1		lg. French bread, cubed
6	T	butter, melted
¾	#	shred. swiss cheese
½	#	monterey jack ch. shred.
9		thin slices Genoa salami
16		eggs
3¼	c	milk
½	c	dry wht. wine
4		grn. onions chop.
1	T	mustard
¼	t	pepper
⅛	t	red pepper
1½	c	sour cream
1	c	parmesan cheese

Spread bread cubes over bottom of 2 buttered 9x13 pans & sprinkle with melted butter. Sprinkle with cheeses & chopped salami. Beat eggs, milk, wine, mustard, onions & peppers till foamy. Pour over cheeses & bread. Cover with foil & refrigerate. Remove 30 min. before placing in 325° oven. Bake covered 1 hr. Uncover & spread with sour cream & parmesan cheese. Bake uncovered till crusty & browned, about 10 min.

Lauren Collins
Schaumburg

"NO-CRUST" QUICHE

1½ c milk
½ c Bisquick
6   T margarine, room temperature
3   eggs
pinch salt

Mix in blender 30-40 seconds. Pour the above into ungreased 9-10" pie pan. Then add 1 c of any of these: diced ham, turkey or bacon, shrimp, 4 oz. can sliced mushrooms or 1 c chopped broccoli. Push the ingredients down into batter. Sprinkle 1 c grated cheese on top (any kind). Bake at 350° for 45-50 min. Let stand 5 min. before serving.

Grace Merrill
Naperville

MEXICAN QUICHE

Press 2 cans of green chili pepper onto bottom of 9" pie plate. Grate 1" sharp cheddar into 6 beaten eggs. Pour over chilis & bake for 25 min. at 350°.

Linda Meldorf
Oak Park

CURRIED CHICKEN & BROCCOLI

6   chicken breasts, cooked & meat taken off
2   pkg. froz. broccoli spears or 1 # fresh cooked lightly & drained
1 c sour cream
1   can cream of chicken soup
1   pkg. shredded cheddar cheese (2 c)
1 c corn flakes
1 t curry
3 T butter

In 9x13 pan layer broccoli, then chicken meat (cut into pieces). Heat soup, sour cream & curry till warm & blended. Pour over chicken. Layer cheddar cheese next. Melt butter & add corn flakes, sprinkle on top of cheese. Bake at 350° for 35-45 min. or till bubbly.

Patti Margaron
Naperville

CHICKEN & BROCCOLI WITH SWISS CHEESE

1½ # fresh broccoli or 2 pkg. frozen
1   chicken, cooked & meat taken off
1   can cream-chicken soup
1   pt. sour cream
¾ # swiss cheese, sliced

Cook & drain broccoli. Place on bottom of buttered 9x13 glass pan. Combine soup & sour cream & put ½ over broccoli. Lay ½ of cheese over sauce. Put sliced chicken next, last ½ of sauce & top with remaining swiss cheese. Sprinkle with paprika. Bake at 400° for 25 min. or till hot & bubbly.

Diane O'Connor
Downers Grove

AU GRATIN CHICKEN BAKE

2	c	chopped cooked chicken or turkey
1		10¾ oz. can cream of celery soup
1		8 oz. can water chestnuts, drain & slice
4		oz. spaghetti, cook & drain
1	c	shredded cheddar cheese
1	c	grated parmesan cheese
½	c	milk
1	T	chopped pimento

Combine chicken, soup, water chestnuts, spaghetti, ½ c cheddar, ½ c parmesan, milk & pimento, mix lightly. Spoon into 1½ qt. buttered casserole. Bake at 350° for 45 min. Top with remaining cheeses & bake till melts. Serves 6-8.

Sheila McCann
Lisle

SAVORY CRESCENT CHICKEN SQUARES

3		oz. cream cheese
2	T	melted butter
2	c	cubed, cooked chicken
¼	t	salt
⅛	t	pepper
2	T	milk
1	T	chop. onions
1	T	chop. pimento
1		8 oz. can Pillsbury crescent rolls
¾	c	crushed seasoned croutons

Blend cream cheese & butter till smooth. Add chicken, salt & pepper, milk, chives & pimento. Mix well. Separate rolls into 4 rectangles & seal perforations. Spoon ½ c mixture into center of each rectangle, pull 4 corners together & seal. Brush top with melted butter & dip in crushed croutons. Bake at 350° for 20-25 min. on ungreased cookie sheet. Makes 4 squares.

Margie Aldridge
Lake Zurich

CHICKEN HOW-SO

4		boned & skinned chicken breasts
2	T	butter
1		can golden mush. soup
½	c	water
1		beef bouillon cube
1	T	soy sauce
1	t	worcestershire
½	t	curry powder
½	t	poppy seed
8		oz. bamboo shoots
½	c	sliced celery
½	c	sliced onion
1		3 oz. can mushrooms

sm. grn. pepper, strips

3	T	dry white wine
3		oz. chow mein noodles

Brown chicken, cut in 1½" strips, in butter. Stir in soup, water, beef cube, soy sauce, worcestershire sauce, curry & poppy seed. Cover & simmer 15 min. Add bamboo shoots, celery, onion & mushrooms. Cover & simmer 10 min. Stir in pepper strips & wine. Simmer 2-3 min. Serve over chow mein noodles.

Marilyn Hallihan
Arlington Heights

LEMON BARBEQUED CHICKEN

2		chickens, quartered
1	c	vegetable oil
½	c	lemon juice
1	T	salt
1	t	paprika
2	t	onion powder
2	t	basil
½	t	thyme
½	t	garlic powder

Place chicken in plastic bags in shallow pans. Combine rest of ingredients & pour half in each bag of chicken & marinate overnight or several hours. Grill outside or bake in oven 1-1½ hours.

Sheila McCann
Lisle

SWEET & SOUR CHICKEN

Mix:

1	bottle Russian salad dressing
1	jar Smuckers apricot preserves
1	pkg. Lipton onion soup mix

Pour over chicken pieces in a baking pan. Bake at 350° for 1½ hours.

James & Helen Chevrier
Villa Park

ONE HOUR CHICKEN CACCIATORE

2	#	chicken parts
2	T	shortening
1		can tomato soup
½	c	chopped onion
¼	c	dry red wine
2		lg. garlic cloves, minced
1	t	oregano
¼	t	salt
½		med. green pepper, in strips

Brown chicken in shortening. Pour off fat. Add remaining ingredients, except pepper strips. Cover & cook over low heat 30 min. Add peppers & cook 15 min. more.

Nancy Caronia
Naperville

BEEFY-CHICKEN CASSEROLE

2		pkg. dried beef
4		chicken breasts, halved & boned
4		slices bacon
1		can mushroom soup
1	c	sour cream

Put dried beef in bottom of buttered casserole & lay boned chicken breasts on top. Salt & pepper. Put one slice of bacon on top of each breast. Combine soup & sour cream, pour over chicken & cover. Bake at 350° for 1½ hours.

Marilyn Ermer
Naperville

APRICOT GLAZED CHICKEN

4	T	vegetable oil
4		sm. zucchini, halved lengthwise
½	#	mushrooms
3		chicken breasts
1	c	Italian green beans
½	c	apricot jam
1	T	vinegar
½	t	salt, ginger, garlic, red pepper flakes

Heat oil in skillet, add chicken & brown. Drain fat & add vegetables to chicken, cook a few minutes. Combine remaining ingredients & pour over chicken & vegetables. Place in baking dish & bake at 350° for 40 min.

Mary Schmitt
Naperville

TOMATO BEEF BAKE

6		oz. med. size noodles
1	#	ground beef
1		med. onion, chopped
2		cloves garlic, minced
3		med. tomatoes, cut in chunks
1		med. green pepper, cut in chunks
¼	c	soy sauce

Cook noodles, brown beef with onion & garlic. Mix in tomatoes, green pepper & soy sauce. Heat to boil. Stir in noodles & pour into 2 qt. baking dish. Bake uncovered for 20 min. at 350°. Can also top with grated cheese.

Sheila McCann
Lisle

RICE-BEEF ROULADE

1   c   fresh bread crumbs
¾   c   rice
1⅔ c   beef broth
1   egg
1   #   ground round
½   c   tomato sauce
½   c   chopped green onion
1   t   salt
⅛   t   pepper
¾   t   oregano
1   c   shredded cheddar cheese

Cook rice in beef broth. Spread ¼ c bread crumbs on sheet of wax paper. In bowl mix beef & ¾ c bread crumbs, egg, ¼ c green onions, ¼ c tomato sauce, salt & pepper. Spread mixture over crumbs on wax paper (12x10), patting meat to cover paper. Mix rice, ¾ c cheese, ¼ t oregano, & green onions (¼ c) & spread over meat leaving 1″ meat edge. Lifting wax paper, roll up jelly roll like, pulling off paper as rolling. Place roll seam side down (pinch ends to seal). Use 12x18 dish & bake 30 min. Mix ¼ c tomato sauce, ½ t oregano & pour over. Top with ¼ c cheese & bake 10 min. longer.

Nancy Suffolk
Glendale Heights

BEEF & POTATO LOAF

Arrange on bottom of greased loaf pan:

4 cups peeled, sliced thinly, raw potatoes

Mix:

1   t   **salt**
1   t   **parsley flakes**
⅛   t   **pepper**
1   t   **chopped onion.**

Sprinkle over potatoes. Spread following mixture next:

1   #   **ground beef**
¾   c   **Milnot**
½   c   **cracker meal or dry oatmeal**
1   t   **salt**
¼   c   **catsup or chili sauce**
⅛   t   **pepper**
¼   c   **chopped onion**

Bake at 350° for 1 hour or till meat is done.

Barb Williams
Highland, Ind.

POTATO-BEEF BAKE

3   lg. potatoes (peeled & sliced)
1   can cheddar cheese soup
3   slices American cheese
¾ c milk
1 # ground beef (cooked & drained)
dash of pepper
1   onion diced

Butter casserole dish. Layer ½ of sliced potatoes on bottom. Scoop on soup. Sprinkle onion over, then add ground beef. Dot with butter. Put remaining potatoes on top. Pour milk over all & top with cheese slices. Cover & bake at 375° for 50-60 min.

Mary Schmitt
Naperville

ITALIAN MEAT LOAF

Mix together:

2   **eggs**
6   **oz. tomato paste**
½ c **cracker crumbs**
½ c **chop. onion**
1½ # **ground beef**
¼ c **chop. green pepper**
¾ t **salt**
dash pepper
2   T **parmesan cheese**

Take ½ of mixture & line bread pan. Then mix 12 oz. cottage cheese, ½ c cracker crumbs, ½ c sliced mushrooms, 1 T parsley, ¼ t oregano. Put filling over & top with rest of beef mixture. Bake at 350° for 70 min. Let stand 10 min. & serve.

Lynn Chlada
Cicero

BARBEQUED MEATBALLS

SAUCE
3   T   ground mustard
2   T   Liquid Smoke
1   T   lemon juice
1   T   vinegar
2   T   worcestershire sauce
1   t   each salt & pepper
1   t   chili powder
2   c   catsup

Mix sauce ingredients & bring to boil. Pour over meatballs & heat but do not boil.

MEATBALLS
2   #   ground beef
salt, pepper, chili powder to taste
1   egg
1   onion finely chopped

Form into small balls & bake at 350° for 10-15 min.

Margie Aldridge
Lake Zurich

HAMBURG CHOP SUEY

1	#	ground beef
2		sm. onions, chopped
¾	c	chopped celery
1		can cream of mushroom soup
1		can cream of chicken soup
¼	c	soy sauce
½	c	uncooked rice
1½	c	boiling water

chow mein noodles

Brown the beef, add onions, celery, soups, soy sauce, rice & water. Heat through & then put in casserole dish, sprinkle chow mein noodles on top. Bake uncovered ½ hour at 350°. You may add mushrooms, if desired. Can be prepared ahead of time.

Judy Oslack
Downers Grove

BEEF & CABBAGE CASSEROLE
(Easy Pigs in the Blanket)

1	#	ground beef, browned
1		med. onion, brown with beef
½		cooked cabbage, sliced thin
1		8 oz. can tomato sauce
1	c	rice, cooked
½		pkg. mozzarella cheese

Layer sliced cooked cabbage in bottom of 9x9″ lightly greased pan. Then place beef, rice and finish with another layer of cabbage. Top with tomato sauce and mozzarella cheese.

Mrs. John Baran
Auburn

QUICK BARBEQUE BEEF

Brown:

1½-2 # ground beef

Bring to boil:

1   c **catsup**
½ c **brown sugar**
½ c **vinegar**
1   t **chili powder**

Add browned beef & add chopped onion if desired & heat. Serve on buns.

Beverly Buck
Dundee

BEER BURGERS

2   slices stale rye bread
½ c beer
2 # ground beef
1   med. onion minced
½ t sage
salt & pepper to taste

Trim crusts from bread, pour beer over & let stand till liquid absorbed. In bowl, mix ground beef, onion, bread & seasonings. Mix lightly but well. Pat into patties & refrigerate for 1 hour to blend flavors. Broil or barbecue. Alcohol cooks away.

Colleen & Rich Poncin
Matteson

PIZZA BURGERS

Brown 1 # ground beef, drain. Season with onion salt. Add small can mushrooms, small can tomato sauce, small can tomato paste, dash tabasco sauce, 1 t worcestershire sauce, ½ t oregano, 1 t garlic salt. Cook over low heat ½ hour. Spread mixture on ½ hamburger bun, top with mozzarella cheese & place under broiler.

Kathy DeWig
Aurora

HARD TIMES HOT DOGS

2   c   chopped frankfurters
2   diced hard-cooked eggs
½   c   grated cheddar cheese
2   T   pickle relish
¼   c   chili sauce
½   t   garlic powder
1   t   prepared mustard
8   split frankfurter rolls

Fill each roll & wrap in foil, securing ends in a tight twist. Place on baking sheet & bake for 15-20 min. at 400°. These packages freeze beautifully, if frozen bake for 30 min.

Nancy Suffolk
Glendale Heights

PASTA POTPOURRI

12   oz. Italian sausage
1   c sliced mushrooms
2   t basil
½   t salt
¼   t garlic powder
2   eggs, beaten
¼   c milk
½   c parmesan cheese
8   oz. spaghetti
¼   c butter or marg.
12   cherry tomatoes, halved

Brown sausage, drain, add mushrooms & saute. Stir in basil, salt & garlic, keep warm. In bowl add eggs, milk & cheese. Cook spaghetti, drain, add butter, then add meat mixture & egg mixture, blend well. Stir in tomatoes & serve.

Maureen Sullivan
Westmont

EASY LASAGNA

1	#	Italian sausage
8		oz. lasagna noodles
2		beaten eggs
2	c	cottage cheese
½	c	parmesan cheese
12		oz. sliced mozzarella
1		qt. spaghetti sauce

Cook noodles, drain & rinse. Combine eggs, cottage cheese, parmesan & cooked meat. In 9x13 pan (greased) layer half of noodles, meat mixture, mozzarella & spaghetti sauce. Repeat layers. Bake uncovered at 375° for 1 hr. 10 min. Sprinkle more parmesan cheese on top. Let cool 10 min. before slicing.

Mary Ellen Brady
Richton Park

GREEN & WHITE LASAGNA

Cook & drain 1 # curly lasagna noodles. Saute 2 medium chopped onions 3 garlic cloves, minced & ½ c pine nuts (optional) in ¼ c butter. Thaw & drain 5 (10 oz.) pkg. chopped spinach, then mix into onion mixture, cooking till dry.

Blend well:

1	#	ricotta cheese
4		green onions chopped
1		egg yolk
3	T	minced parsley

Spread each lasagna noodle with thin layers of spinach & ricotta mixture. Jelly roll each noodle & tuck a small stalk of broccoli in each. Put in buttered 9x13 pan & sprinkle with grated parmesan cheese (also optional, gruyere & fontinella cheeses). Can refrigerate or freeze here. When ready to bake, pour Italian cooking sauce over & bake at 375° for 45-60 min.

Diane O'Connor
Downers Grove

SAUSAGE LASAGNA WRAPS

Cook & drain 6 lasagna noodles. Divide 1 # smoked sausage into 6 pieces, split lengthwise & stuff with ½ slice of mozzarella cheese. Wrap each sausage in a lasagna noodle. Place in baking dish & pour 16 oz. jar of Italian cooking sauce over top. Bake at 350° for 30 min. Serve with grated parmesan cheese.

Mary Schmitt
Naperville

VEGETABLES AND SIDE DISHES

WEE COOK

CAULIFLOWER POLONAISE

1   medium fresh cauliflower
½   c   melted butter
1   c   fresh bread crumbs
1   hard cooked egg
2   t   chopped parsley

Cook cauliflower till tender. Drain & place in a serving dish. Melt the butter in a frying pan and brown in it the bread crumbs. Add the hard cooked egg, chopped fine, & the parsley. Season with salt & pepper. Pour over the cauliflower & serve hot.

Rose Bagley
Naperville

CHEESY BROCCOLI BAKE

3   c   or 2 (10 oz.) pkg. broccoli, cook & drain
¼   c   butter or margarine
¼   c   flour
½   t   salt
¾   c   milk
1   c   shredded cheddar cheese
1   sliced tomato
parmesan cheese

In medium pan, melt butter, add flour & salt, mix well. Gradually stir in milk & cheese. Heat till sauce is thick & cheese is melted. Pour over broccoli in 1½ qt. baking dish. Bake 350° for 20 min. or till bubbly. Arrange sliced tomato over cheese, continue baking for 5 min. Sprinkle with parmesan cheese.

Sheila McCann
Lisle

BEHIHANA ZUCCHINI

6   medium zucchini sliced into 4" strips
1   sweet onion sliced
½   #   fresh mushrooms sliced
sesame seeds (about ¾ c)
soy sauce
peanut oil

Heat small amount of oil in pan, brown onion. Add zucchini, sprinkle sesame seeds on. Add mushrooms. Sprinkle soy sauce, cook to desired firmness of zucchini. Strips of sirloin or pork may be added.

Joanne McDonnell
Oakbrook Terrace

MARINATED CARROTS

2   # carrots
small bottle cocktail onions
⅓ c vegetable oil
1 t mustard
1 T worcestershire sauce
1   green pepper sliced
1   can tomato soup
¾ c vinegar
½ c sugar
salt & pepper to taste

Slice & cook carrots. Mix remaining ingredients & pour over carrots while they are still hot. Refrigerate for at least two days. Keep for 2-3 weeks. Can be served hot or cold.

Mary Schmitt
Naperville

CONNECTICUT CARROTS

8-10   carrots
¼   c   chopped parsley
1   small onion, sliced thin

Peel & cut carrots into ¼ - ½ inch slices. Cook in boiling water till just tender. Drain & cool & mix with onion and parsley. Marinate several hours or overnight in the following mixture:

½   c   salad oil
½   c   vinegar
1   t   salt
1   t   pepper
1   t   caraway seed
1   t   celery seed or salt
½   t   garlic powder

Cindy Fischer
Frankfort

SWISS SQUASH BAKE

½ c butter
1½ c sliced zucchini or yellow summer squash
1½ c cut fresh broccoli or 1 pkg. 10 oz. frozen, thawed & cut
1   egg
½ c shredded swiss cheese
1 t salt
¼ t dry mustard
dash cayene pepper
¼ c grated parmesan cheese
¼ c milk

Melt butter in large skillet. Add vegetables & cook till tender. Beat egg slightly, stir in swiss cheese, milk, salt, mustard & pepper. Place vegetables in 1 qt. baking dish. Pour egg mixture over vegetables, sprinkle with parmesan cheese. Bake at 375° for 15-20 min.

Diane O'Connor
Downers Grove

POTATOES ROMANOFF

8		medium potatoes
2	c	sour cream
6		green onions sliced (only some of green)
2½	c	shredded cheddar cheese
1¼	t	salt
¼	t	pepper
paprika		

Cook potatoes in jackets till tender (but not too soft). Peel & shred. Combine potatoes, sour cream, 2 c cheese, sliced green onions, salt & pepper. Turn mixture into a buttered 9x13 pan. Sprinkle wth ½ c cheese & paprika. Refrigerate, if desired, till time to bake. Bake at 350° for 30-40 min.

Diane O'Connor
Downers Grove

ALMOND POTATO PUFF

4   lg. potatoes
3   eggs, separated
1 t salt
1   very small onion grated
2 T butter melted
½ c blanched almonds

Cook potatoes till done. Peel & mash well. Stir in egg yolks, salt & onion. Beat egg whites till stiff. Fold into potato mixture. Spoon carefully into deep greased casserole. Drizzle with melted butter & sprinkle with almonds. This may be prepared in advance, refrigerated & then baked just before serving. Bake 350° for 30 min. Don't open oven door till done. Serves 6-8.

Marilyn Hallihan
Arlington Heights

POTATO CASSEROLE

2 # frozen hash brown potatoes
½ c melted butter
1 t salt
¼ t pepper
½ c chopped onion
1 c sour cream
2 c grated cheddar cheese
1   can cream of chicken soup

Mix all together. Top with 2 c crushed corn flakes & ¼ c melted butter.
Bake in 9″x13″ pan, 45 min. Or use 2 smaller pans & freeze one for later
use. Cut baking time to 30 min. for smaller pan. Bake at 350°.

Nancy Caronia
Naperville

SPAGHETTI SQUASH

Cut squash in half, remove seeds. Bake, cut side down, in baking pan containing small amount of water at 350° for 45 min. After cooking, pull strands free with a fork, toss with small amount of margarine and season to taste.

Diane O'Connor
Downers Grove

BAKED RICE WITH TOASTED PINE NUTS

2	T	butter or margarine
½	c	finely chopped onion
1	t	finely minced garlic
1	c	rice
1½	c	chicken broth
1		bay leaf

Melt ½ of the butter in a pan, add onion & garlic. Cook till onion wilts.
Add rice & stir. Add broth & bay leaf & cover. Heat to boil & then bake for
exactly 17 min. (or can finish cooking over low heat on stove). Remove
bay leaf, add remaining butter and toasted pine nuts & 2 T parsley.
Serves 4. To toast ¼ c pine nuts: cook in a small skillet stirring & shaking
till they brown. Recipe can be increased as much as needed.

Diane O'Connor
Downers Grove

RICE & MUSHROOMS

1   c rice
2   cans onion soup
1   stick margarine
1   can mushrooms

Saute mushrooms in melted margarine. Add rice and soup. Bake at 325°
for 1 hour.

Robin Biesen
New Lenox

WILD RICE CASSEROLE

1 c wild rice
2   cans consomme
½ # mushrooms
1 T butter
½ c chopped celery
½ c chopped onion
salt & pepper to taste

Wash rice in strainer then place in 1½ qt. casserole covered with boiling water & allow to stand for ½ hour or more. Add 1 can consomme, salt, pepper, onion & celery & let soak for 3 hours. Saute mushrooms in butter & add to casserole. Bake at 350° for 1½ - 2 hours adding more consomme as needed. Serves 4-6.

Diane House
Deerfield

GARDEN SKILLET

⅓   c   uncooked rice
3   T   butter
2   c   thinly sliced zucchini
1   c   thinly sliced carrots
½   c   water
1   t   salt
½   t   garlic powder
¼   c   grated parmesan cheese

Cook rice, set aside. In medium saucepan melt butter. Add zucchini & carrots & cook, stirring 5 minutes. Add water & cook until vegetables are tender. Add rice, salt, garlic, 2 T parmesan cheese & stir. Turn into serving dish & sprinkle with remaining cheese.

Janet Dick
Naperville

QUICK PICNIC BEANS

Brown:

1   #   **ground beef**
1   **chopped onion**

Mix in:

1   c   **catsup**
1   T   **dry mustard**
¼   c   **brown sugar**
salt & pepper to taste
2   **1 # cans pork and beans**

Put in casserole & bake at 325° for one hour.

Kathy DeWig
Aurora

THREE BEAN CASSEROLE

4		strips bacon, fried & crumbled
1		12 oz. can pork & beans with tomato sauce
1		pkg. frozen baby limas, cooked & drained
1		can red kidney beans or butter beans
1		medium onion, chopped & browned
¼	c	brown sugar
¼	c	catsup
¼	#	Velveeta, cubed

Mix all ingredients (include only some of the tomato sauce with the pork & beans). Put in 1¾ qt. casserole & bake for 30 min.

Marilyn Hallihan
Arlington Heights

VEGETABLE CASSEROLE

1		can drained green beans
1		can drained wax beans
2	c	canned tomatoes plus juice
½	c	purple skin onions, sliced in rings
1½	c	carrot strips, cut thick - 2" long
2	c	celery strips, cut thick - 2" long
¾	c	green pepper strips
4	T	butter
1½	T	sugar
3	T	minute tapioca
⅛	t	pepper
2½	t	salt

Mix well in greased casserole. Cover & bake at 350° for 2 hours.

James & Helen Chevrier
Villa Park

CRANBERRIES GRAND MARINER

2   c   sugar
2   c   water
1   #   cranberries
3   T   Grand Mariner
grated rind one orange
juice of ½ lemon

Combine sugar & water, boil five min. Add cranberries, boil 5 min. more until almost jelled. Fold in remaining ingredients. Remove from heat. Sprinkle with 2 additional T sugar. Fold in sugar - chill. A super accompaniment to any entree. Can be frozen.

Jane O'Hare
Downers Grove

SWEETS

N.SUFFOLK

CHOCOLATE ECLAIR CAKE

1   box graham crackers
1   8 oz. container frozen whipped topping
2   boxes instant French vanilla pudding mix
3½ c milk

Mix pudding & milk well. Blend in whipped topping. Butter a 9x13 pan.
Layer graham crackers on bottom, next half of pudding mix, another
layer of crackers, and rest of pudding, finish with crackers. Frost with the
following frosting:

FROSTING:
2   sq. semi-sweet chocolate (or 6 T cocoa & 2 T oil)
1½ c powdered sugar
1 t vanilla
2 T white corn syrup
3 T milk
3 T melted butter

Frost cake and chill at least 12 hours, better if made day ahead.

Nancy Suffolk
Glendale Heights

OATMEAL CAKE

1 c oatmeal
1 c shortening
1⅓ c boiling water

Mix first 3 ingredients & let stand 20 min., stirring several times. Add the following ingredients:

½ t cinnamon
½ t salt
1 t soda
1 c brown sugar
1 c white sugar
2   eggs
1⅓ c flour

Bake at 350° for 45 min., in a 9x13 pan.

TOPPING
¼ c melted butter
4 T milk
1 c brn. sugar
1 c coconut
1 c chopped nuts

Mix & spread on cake. Broil until brown right before serving.

Kathleen Waller
Downers Grove

NANCY'S COLA CAKE

2   c   flour
2   c   sugar
1   c   margarine or butter
1   c   cola beverage
3   T   cocoa
½   c   buttermilk
2   eggs beaten
1   t   vanilla
1½ c   miniature marshmallows

Combine flour & sugar in bowl. Melt butter; add cola & cocoa & heat to boiling. Pour over flour & sugar & beat thoroughly. Add buttermilk, eggs, soda, vanilla & marshmallows. Bake in a greased & floured 9x13 pan at 350° for 30-35 minutes.

COLA CAKE ICING
½   c   butter
6   T   cola beverage
3   T   cocoa
2   c   powdered sugar
1   c   chopped pecans

Combine butter, cola, & cocoa & heat to boiling. Pour over powdered sugar & beat well. Add pecans. Ice cake while it's warm.

Nancy Suffolk
Glendale Heights

BUTTER PECAN ICE CREAM CAKE

1		pkg. Lorna Doone Cookies
1		stick butter
2		pkg. instant vanilla pudding
2	c	milk
2		pts. butter pecan ice cream

cool whip

Crush cookies in 9x13 pan, pour melted butter over, mix & pat down as crust. Whip together pudding, milk & ice cream. Pour over crust & frost with cool whip. Let set for at least 2 hrs. in refrigerator.

Cindy Fischer
Frankfort

GOOEY BUTTER CAKE

1   yellow cake mix
1   stick margarine melted
1   egg

Mix these together & press on bottom of 9x13 pan.

1   8 oz. cream cheese
2   eggs
1 # box powdered sugar
1 t vanilla

Blend these ingredients for 3 min. & pour over the first mixture. Bake 20 min. at 350°. Sprinkle with chopped nuts & return to oven for another 20 min. till golden.

Marilyn Ermer
Naperville

CHOCOLATE ZUCCHINI CAKE

½   c   **margarine**
½   c   **oil**
1¾ c   **sugar**

Cream the above ingredients and then add:

2   **eggs**
1   t   **vanilla**
½   c   **sour milk**

Sift & add:

2½ c   **flour**
4   T   **cocoa**
½   t   **baking powder**
1   t   **baking soda**

Add last:

2   c   **grated zucchini**

Put in greased 9x13 pan & top with ¼ c chocolate chips. Bake for 40-45 min. Serve with whipped cream or ice cream. (Set oven at 350°.)

Diane Klopp
Naperville

"REAL" BANANA CAKE

1 box Regular Yellow Cake mix, use:

¼ c *less* water per cake mix directions
1 c fresh mashed bananas
⅛ t soda
½ c chopped nuts

IRISH MINT FROSTING

Blend:

¼ t peppermint extract
3 drops green food coloring
2 c thawed cool whip

Frost top of 2, 8″ cake layers or top & sides of an 8″ square cake. Garnish with mint leaves & chocolate curls.

Nancy Suffolk
Glendale Heights

BANANA SPLIT CAKE

1st layer:
2   c crushed graham crackers   ½ c melted butter

Mix & press in bottom of 9x13 pan.

2nd layer:
2   sticks soft butter   2   c powdered sugar
2   eggs   1   t vanilla

Beat till firm & spread on above.

3rd layer:
3   large bananas sliced & dipped in pineapple juice

4th layer:
1   can drained crushed pineapple

5th layer:
1   lg. cool whip or whipping cream

6th layer: sprinkle with —
chopped nuts   **maraschino cherries**

Chill 8 hours . . . . . . it's dee-licious!

Nancy Suffolk
Glendale Heights

RHUBARB CAKE

2   c diced rhubarb
½   c sugar
½   c shortening
1½   c sugar
1   egg
2   c flour
1   t soda
1   c sour milk
dash salt
1   t cinnamon
1   t vanilla

Mix rhubarb with ½ c sugar & let stand. Cream shortening, 1½ c sugar, egg & then add sifted dry ingredients alternately with the sour milk. Add vanilla. When batter is mixed, add rhubarb & blend. Bake 1 hour at 350° in a greased & floured 9x13 pan. Serve plain, with whipped cream or ice cream.

Diane Klopp
Naperville

COWBOY CAKE

1   c   margarine
2   c   flour
1½ c   brown sugar
1   c   sour milk (1 t vinegar or lemon juice to milk)
1   egg
1   t   soda
1   t   vanilla

Mix flour, sugar & butter till crumbles. Take out ⅔ c for icing. Add baking soda to milk. Add egg, milk & vanilla to first mixture. Mix well & pour into a 9x13 greased & floured pan. Sprinkle ⅔ of topping over cake & ½ c nuts. Bake at 350° for 30 min.

Jan LeMonnier
Frankfort

ANGEL BAVARIAN CAKE

1   pt. milk
4   egg yolks
1   c   sugar
2   T   flour
pinch of salt
rum to taste or vanilla

Cook all of the above till creamy & custardy.

Dissolve 1 pkg. unflavored gelatine in ½ c cold water. Put this into hot custard, mix & let cool very well.

Fold in 1 pt. whipped cream & 4 beaten egg whites. Break into pieces 1 pkg. angel food cake & line pan with pieces. Layer with custard & then repeat. Let stand overnight in frig. When ready to serve turn cake on plate & frost with ½ pt. of whipped cream. Sprinkle with coconut and garnish with strawberries if desired. Use angel food or bundt cake pan.

Mary Grace Butler
Oak Park

EASY & DELICIOUS PINEAPPLE CAKE

2   c   sugar
2   c   flour
¼   c   chopped nuts
2   t   baking soda
1   T   vanilla
2   eggs
1   20 oz. can crushed pineapple (not drained)

Mix all above ingredients till blended, mix by hand. Butter 9x13 pan. Bake at 350° for 40 min. Frost with the following icing:

ICING:
2   c   powdered sugar
8   oz. cream cheese
1   stick butter or margarine
1   t   vanilla

Blend together & frost.

MaryAnn O'Brien
Frankfort

JEWELED FRUIT CAKE

2   eggs
½   c   water
1   jar None Such Rum & Brandy Mince Meat
2   pkgs. date & nut bread mix
2   c   mixed candied fruit
1   c   chopped nuts

Combine eggs & water. Stir in other ingredients & mix well. Turn batter into greased & floured 10″ tube or bundt pan. Bake 80-90 min. till toothpick comes out clean. Cool 15 min. & turn out onto rack to finish cooling. Drizzle with powdered sugar glaze if desired. Wrap cake in foil & refrigerate. Can be stored a long time. Bake at 350°.

Catherine Ellis
Hobart, Indiana

ALMOND LOVERS CAKE

1   **box Pillsbury Plus Yellow Cake Mix**
1   **can Solo brand almond paste**
¾   **stick butter**
3   **eggs**
1¼ c **water**

Put all of above in large mixing bowl, mix at medium speed for 2 min., then mix at high speed for an extra 2 min. Bake in tube pan for 1 hour (grease & flour pan). When cake is done immediately invert onto cake plate. Make cake drizzle with 2½ c powdered sugar, 1 t vanilla & enough water to make a glaze. Glaze cake while still warm, making certain to cover all of cake. Quickly sprinkle almond slivers on top as glaze hardens fast. Cool before cutting.

Jane Davis
Lombard

BEET RED CHOCOLATE CAKE

3   eggs
1½ c   sugar
1   c   oil
1½ c   grated cooked beets (may use canned)
2   oz. melted chocolate
1¾ c   flour
1½ t   baking soda
½   t   salt
1   t   vanilla

Beat eggs with sugar till light. Add oil, beets & melted chocolate. Mix well. Sift flour with soda & salt. On low speed of mixer add dry ingred. Add vanilla. Pour batter into a greased & floured 9″ tube pan. Bake at 350° for 50-60 min. Cool cake in pan on rack for 10 min. Take out and cool completely before frosting or dusting with powdered sugar. Very moist & delicious.

James & Helen Chevrier
Villa Park

CHEESE CAKE

2   pkgs. crescent rolls
2   lg. cream cheese
1   egg yolk
1   egg white
¾ c sugar
2 t vanilla

Grease a 9x13 pan. Put 1 pkg. rolls over bottom of pan. Blend cheese, sugar, egg yolk & vanilla. Spread over bottom crust. Top with remaining rolls & brush top with beaten egg whites. Bake at 350° for 30 min. Top with powdered sugar.

Denise Bell
Schaumburg

GERMAN CHOCOLATE CHEESE CAKE

1½ c graham cracker crumbs
3 T sugar
9 oz. cream cheese
¾ c sugar
dash salt
⅓ c butter
vanilla to taste
2 oz. semi-sweet chocolate, melted
2 eggs
3 T butter
5 T evaporated milk
½ c brown sugar
½ c coconut & pecans, chopped

Make crust with grahams, sugar & butter & press into bottom of greased 9″ cake pan. Beat cream cheese, sugar & salt until smooth. Add melted chocolate & mix well. Add eggs one at a time while mixing. Add vanilla & pour into cake pan till ½ full. Bake at 325° for 45 min. or till toothpick comes out clean. Melt 3 T butter in evaporated milk, stir in brown sugar & cook till melted. Add chopped nuts & coconut. Pour over baked cake & refrigerate till firm.

Judy Pease
Hinsdale

PEACH PIE

1   c   crushed graham crackers
1   T   sugar
½   c   melted butter

Mix above ingredients & pat into 9-10″ pie shell. Melt ½ # marshmallows in ½ c milk (use a double boiler or watch closely). Cool & then fold in ½ pint whipped whipping cream. (Can use cool whip.) Then fold in 3 finely diced or sliced fresh peaches, (can use more fruit if desired or other type of fruit). Pour into crust & refrigerate 8 hours or overnight.

Patti Kulpinski
Palatine

CHOCOLATE PECAN PIE

1	c	sugar
4	T	cornstarch
2		eggs, lightly beaten
½	c	butter or marg., melted & cooled
3	T	bourbon *or* 1 t vanilla
6		oz. pkg. semisweet chocolate chips
1	c	finely chopped pecans
1		9″ unbaked pie shell

whipped cream

Combine sugar & cornstarch in medium size bowl & beat in eggs. Then mix in butter, bourbon or vanilla, chocolate chips & pecans. Pour into pie shell. Bake at 350° for 40 min. or till puffy & lightly browned. Cool & cut into slim pieces (it is very rich). Top with whipped cream.

Lauren Collins
Schaumburg

FUDGE PIE

Melt 1 sq. chocolate & ¼ # butter or margarine. Cool, then add:

1	c	sugar
2		eggs slightly beaten
1		scant cup sifted flour (one tablespoon take out)
1	T	vanilla

Mix well & pour into greased pie plate. Bake for 25 min. at 350°. Check after 20 min., should be soft inside. Serve with whipped cream or ice cream.

Jane Davis
Lombard

FRENCH SILK PIE

1	c	sugar
¾	c	butter, cut up *Do not use margarine*
3		sq. unsweetened chocolate melted & cool
1½	t	vanilla
3		eggs
1		pastry shell, baked & cooled

whipped cream
chocolate curls

Blend sugar & butter till very smooth & light. Add chocolate & vanilla & continue mixing. Add eggs, one at a time till mixture is smooth & then turn into cooled pie shell. Chill several hours or overnight. Garnish with whipped cream & curls if desired. Forget the calorie charts & just enjoy!

Ann Bagley
Naperville

LEMON SPONGE PIE

1 c sugar
2 T butter
2   egg yolks
2 T flour

Mix these ingredients well and add:

Juice & grated rind of one lemon
1 c milk

Fold in 2 well-beaten egg whites. Pour into unbaked pie shell. Bake at 450° for 10 min. and then 325° for 30-40 min.

Jan Miller
Naperville

SIMPLE & GREAT ICE CREAM PUFFS

COCONUT CRUST FOR PIES:
Combine 3—3½ oz. cans (4 cups) flaked coconut & 6 T melted butter.
Press on bottom & sides of two 9″ pie plates. Bake at 325° for 20 min. or
till edges are golden brown. Cool before filling.

1. Lime sherbet scooped into pie shell with creame de menthe over top.

2. Banana Split - vanilla ice cream scoops with sliced banana, chocolate
   sauce, peanuts & dabs of whipped cream.

3. Vanilla ice cream scoops with fresh peaches or strawberries over.

I make the crust & fill pie with ice cream scoops a day ahead, then add the
toppings just before serving.

Marlene Herrling
Woodbridge, Va.

STRAWBERRY-APPLE TART

4		medium cooking apples
¼	c	sugar
¼	t	cinnamon
¼	t	nutmeg
⅔		stick butter

pie crust in 10″ tart or pie pan

Peel apples & slice into thin wedges. Sprinkle a little sugar, cinnamon & nutmeg over prepared pie crust. Arrange apples in circle overlapping neatly. Dice leftover apples & place in middle & around edges where spaces are. Again sprinkle over the top the sugar, cinnamon, nutmeg mixture. Cut the butter into pieces & spread evenly over apples. Bake at 400° for 45 min. When cool glaze the pie with ¼ c orange marmalade & 2 T butter melted. Mix over low heat till well blended. Spoon over apples & then slice strawberries & place neatly around outer edge.

Ron Boyd, ICF photographer
Chicago

BONNIE'S TRASCHMANIAN APPLE DESSERT

4   c   chopped unpeeled apples
½   c   apple cider or juice
¼   c   honey
1   t   vanilla
1   t   cinnamon
⅛   t   nutmeg
⅛   t   cloves
½   c   whole wheat flour
⅔   c   milk
2   eggs beaten

Combine all ingredients in a deep oven dish. Place dish in cold oven &
then turn on to 375° & bake for 45-50 min. till apples are tender. Serve
with fresh cream & wild gypsy music.

Bonnie Koloc
New York & Chicago

APPLE CHEESE PANDOWDY

6   c   pared sliced cooking apples
1   c   shredded cheddar cheese
½   c   sugar
1   t   cinnamon
½   t   salt
¼   t   nutmeg

Turn into a buttered 1½ qt. casserole. To prepare crust, combine 1¼ c bisquit mix & 1 T sugar. Stir in ¼ c milk & 2 T melted butter. Roll out ¼" thick and large enough to allow a small overlap around edge of dish. Cut slits so steam can escape. Bake 325° for 50 min. Serve with ice cream or sour cream.

Jan LeMonnier
Frankfort

CRANBERRY STEAMED PUDDING

4   c   cranberries, frozen, chopped
3   c   flour
½   t   salt
½   c   corn syrup
½   c   molasses
4   t   baking soda
⅔   c   hot water

Mix all ingredients, first dry, then wet. Steam for 1½ hours. To steam use small loaf pans or 1# coffee tins (4 or 5 for the recipe). Fill buttered tins or pans ¾ full. Place them in a pan of water and bake in 350° oven.

Serve hot with butter sauce: Heat 2 c sugar, ½ c butter & 1 c cream till butter melts, add 1 t vanilla. Serve over hot pudding, cut into individual slices.

Mary Ellen Durbin
Lisle

BLUEBERRY COBBLER

4 c blueberries
3 T lemon juice
1½ c sugar
6 T butter
1 c milk
2 c flour
2 t baking powder
½ t salt
1 c sugar
2 T cornstarch
1 t salt
1½ c boiling water

Put berries in 9x13 pan and sprinkle with lemon juice. Cream sugar & butter, add flour, baking powder & salt, then milk. Pour over berries. Combine sugar, cornstarch & salt. Sprinkle over top of batter. Pour boiling water over all. Bake at 400° for 45 min.

Pat Owens
Chicago

BLUEBERRY SURPRISE

CRUST
2   c   crushed graham crackers
1   stick butter melted

Press into 8x8 pan & bake at 350° for 10 min. & cool.

Mix:

1   lg. pkg. cream cheese
1   c   powdered sugar
2   T   milk

Spread on crust.

Top with 1 c chopped walnuts & 1-2 c blueberries. Frost with whipped cream or cool whip. (Option, you can use pie filling instead of blueberries.)

Marilyn Ermer
Naperville

EASY PUMPKIN SLICES

4		eggs
2	c	sugar
1		can pumpkin (not filling)
2	c	flour
1	c	oil
2	t	baking powder
1	t	baking soda
¾	t	salt
2	t	cinnamon
¼	t	cloves

Mix all ingredients and pour into 10x15 greased pan. Bake at 350° for 20-25 min.

FROSTING
3		oz. pkg. cream cheese
¾		stick margarine
1	T	milk
1	t	vanilla
1½-2	c	powdered sugar

Beat till smooth & frost cake when cool.

Denise Bell
Schaumburg

PUMPKIN DELIGHT

1   pkg. yellow cake mix (reserve one cup)
½ c butter or margarine melted
1   egg

Mix together & grease bottom of 9x13 pan. Press cake mixture into bottom of pan.

FILLING
1 # (14 oz.) can of pumpkin mix or 3 c.
2   eggs
⅔ c milk

Mix together & pour pumpkin mixture over crust.

TOPPING
1 c reserved cake mix
¼ c sugar
1 t cinnamon
¼ c butter or margarine

Mix together till crumbly & sprinkle over filling. Bake at 350° for 45-50 min. or till knife comes out clean. Use whipped topping when serving.

Mary Ellen Durbin
Lisle

CORN FLAKE COOKIES

,colate
,er chocolate
,ed corn flakes

1   `   ,

Melt chocolates together. Stir in flakes & nuts. Drop by teaspoonful on wax paper & chill.

Robin Biesen
New Lenox

BUCKEYE COOKIES

½   #   margarine or butter
1   #   powdered sugar
1   c   peanut butter
½   #   crushed graham crackers
1   t   vanilla
12   oz. pkg. chocolate chips

Cream margarine & sugar. Add rest of ingredients & mix well. Roll in small balls & lay on waxed paper. Chill several hours. Melt chocolate chips & a 1″ to 2″ piece of paraffin in double boiler & dip the balls. Place back on waxed paper to set.

Lauren Collins
Schaumburg

ANGEL COOKIES

½ c sugar
½ c brown sugar
1 c shortening
2 c flour
1 t baking soda
1 t cream of tartar
1   egg
½ c coconut
½ t salt
1 t vanilla

Cream butter, sugar & vanilla. Mix dry ingredients & add to the mixture. Make into balls & place on cookie sheet. Flatten balls with greased bottom of a glass dipped in sugar. Bake at 400° for 8-10 min. till lightly browned.

Carol Clark
Naperville

BUTTER TURTLE COOKIES

2 c butter
1½ c sugar
3 t cream or milk
2   egg yolks
2 t vanilla
4 c flour
pinch baking soda
walnut or pecan halves
1   lg. Hershey bar melted

Cream butter & sugar, add egg, vanilla & cream. Mix well. Add flour. Roll mixture into balls, about ½ t. Place on ungreased cookie sheet. Add nuts for feet of turtles. Bake at 350° for about 10 min. or till lightly browned. Spread melted chocolate on top of cookie. Makes about 8 doz.

Jan LeMonnier
Frankfort

TOFFEE BUTTER BAR COOKIES

1	c	butter
1	c	brown sugar
1		egg
1	t	vanilla
2	c	flour
8		milk chocolate bars
¼	c	chopped nuts

Cream butter & sugar, add egg, beat till light. Add vanilla & flour & blend thoroughly. Spread in small cookie sheet & bake at 350° for 15-20 min. While hot spread milk bars on top. Sprinkle with chopped nuts.

Maribeth O'Malley
Hoffman Estates

PECAN FINGERS

1	c	butter or margarine
¼	c	powdered sugar
¼	t	salt
1	t	vanilla
1	t	water
2	c	sift. flour
1	c	pecans, chopped

sm. bowl of powdered sugar for rolling cooled cookies

Cream butter, blend in sugar, salt, vanilla & water. Add flour & nuts. Pinch off about ¾ t & roll into finger shape. Place on ungreased cookie sheet. Bake at 350° for 12-15 min.

Jan Henry
Lockport

SCOTCH SHORTBREAD COOKIES

½ # butter
¾ c rice flour
1½ c flour
¾ c powdered sugar

Sift all dry ingredients over softened butter. Work together well. Press onto cookie sheet. Sprinkle with sugar. Bake at 275° for one hour. Cut into squares or strips immediately after coming out of oven.

Rose Bagley
Naperville

RITZ COOKIES
Super Simple & Delicious!

Sandwich Ritz crackers & peanut butter. Melt almond bark & chocolate chips. Dip crackers and place on wax paper.

Marilyn Ermer
Naperville

BEST EVER BROWNIES
FROM A METHODIST CHURCH
COOK BOOK IN DEER RIVER, MINNESOTA

½ c butter or margarine
1 c sugar
1   16 oz. can Hersheys chocolate syrup
1 c plus 1 T flour
½ c chopped nuts
4   eggs beaten
½ t salt
(no baking soda or powder needed in this recipe)

Cream butter & sugar, add eggs & mix well. Add chocolate syrup, flour, salt & nuts. Bake in 9x13 pan at 350° for 25-30 min.

FROSTING
6 T each milk & butter
1½ c sugar
¾ c chocolate chips
1 t vanilla

Mix together in sauce pan & bring to rolling boil for ½ min., **no more.** Remove from heat, add choc. chips & vanilla & stir to blend & chips melted. Put this pan into another pan which has cold water in it, & stir to desired thickness for spreading.

Bonnie's Aunt Clara
Iowa

ZUCCHINI BARS

4   eggs
2 c sugar
1½ c oil
2 c shredded zucchini
2 t vanilla
2 c flour
½ t salt
2 t baking soda
2 t cinnamon
¾ c chopped nuts

Combine grated zucchini, oil, sugar & beat in eggs. Sift dry ingredients & add to zucchini. Then add vanilla & nuts. Pour into greased & floured 9x13 pan. Bake at 350° for 45 min. Frost with cream cheese frosting when cool.

CREAM CHEESE FROSTING

6   oz. cream cheese
2 c powdered sugar
2 t vanilla

Beat until smooth.

Paula Schumacher
Naperville

REESE'S BARS

2½   sticks margarine
12   oz. chocolate chips
1½ c peanut butter
2½ c powdered sugar
1½ c graham cracker crumbs

Melt 1½ sticks margarine with 1½ c peanut butter. Stir in cracker crumbs & 2½ c powdered sugar. Mixture will be very thick. Spread into a 9x13 pan & press smooth. Melt chocolate chips & 1 stick margarine & pour over. Refrigerate.

Sheryl Ginaven
Gary, Ind.

OATMEAL BARS

1   c   butter or margarine
1   c   brown sugar
3   c   quick oatmeal
2   t   vanilla
pinch of salt

Melt butter & add the other ingredients. Press on the bottom of a 9x13 pan. Bake at 375° for 8 min. Cool.

TOPPING
½   c   peanut butter
1   c   chocolate chips

Melt the 2 ingredients in a double boiler & spread over oatmeal crust. Cool & cut. We like them frozen.

Kathleen Waller
Downers Grove

CARAMEL PECAN BARS

⅔ c margarine
½ c packed brn. sugar
1½ c flour
28   Kraft caramels
¼ c water
¼ c margarine
2   eggs, beaten
¼ c sugar
½ t vanilla
¼ t salt
1 c chopped pecans

Cream margarine & sugar till light, add flour & mix well. Press onto bottom of 9x13 pan. Bake at 375° for 15 min. Melt caramels with water & margarine in pan over low heat. Stir till smooth. Combine eggs, sugar, vanilla & salt. Gradually add caramel sauce, mix well. Stir in pecans. Pour over crust. Continue baking 15 min. Cool.

Maureen Sullivan
Westmont

TURTLE BARS

2 c flour
1 c packed brown sugar
½ c butter
1½ c pecan halves

TOPPING
½ c packed brown sugar
⅔ c butter
1 bag milk chocolate chips

Mix flour, sugar & butter till crumbly. Press into ungreased 9x13 pan. Sprinkle pecans over.

For topping cook sugar & butter in pan, stirring constantly till mixture begins to boil. Boil 1 min., pour over pecans. Bake at 350° for 20-25 min. till firm. Immediately sprinkle chips over baked mixture. Spread to cover & cool completely.

Donna T. Bos
Frankfort

CHOCOLATE CRUNCHY BAR

½ c butter
¼ c sugar
2   eggs
1 t vanilla
¾ c flour
½ c chopped nuts
2 T cocoa
¼ t baking powder
2 c tiny marshmallows
1   16 oz. pkg. chocolate chips
1 c peanut butter
1½ c Rice Krispies

Cream butter & sugar, beat in eggs & vanilla. Stir dry ingredients & ¼ t salt. Spread on bottom of greased 9x13 pan and bake at 350° for 15-20 min. Sprinkle marshmallows on top & bake 3 more min. Cool. In small pan combine chips & peanut butter & stir over low heat till chocolate is melted. Stir in Rice Krispies. Spread on bars. Chill.

Diane Klopp
Naperville

SPECIAL K BARS

1   c   white corn syrup
1   c   white sugar

Mix in dutch oven & just bring to boil. Add:

½   c   peanut butter
2   t   vanilla
8   c   Special K cereal

Mix well & press into ungreased 9x13 pan. Spread the following topping over bars: (melt over hot water)

2   T   shortening
½   c   chocolate chips
1   12 oz. pkg. butterscotch chips

Marilyn Ermer
Naperville

LITTLE CREAM CHEESE CAKES

1¾"   diameter baking cups
2   8 oz. pkg. cream cheese
2   eggs
¾ c sugar
1 t vanilla
Keebler vanilla wafers
1   can fruit pie filling

Place wafer in bottom of baking cup. Mix ¾ c sugar, eggs & cream cheese with mixer. Pour into baking cups. Bake 10 min. at 350°. Then add fruit topping & chill. Makes about 32.

MaryAnn O'Brien
Frankfort

NUT CUPS

3   oz. pkg. cream cheese
½   c   butter
1   c   flour
dash of salt

Form into little balls & press into small cupcake tins.

¾   c   dark brown sugar
1   T   metled butter
1   egg
1   c   chopped walnuts

Pour into shells & bake at 350° for 20-25 min. or till golden brown. Makes 2 doz.

Mary Schmitt
Naperville

EASY-DO DOUGHNUTS

⅓ c sugar
½ c milk
1   egg
2 T melted shortening
1½ c flour
2 t baking powder
½ t salt
⅛ t nutmeg
½ c raisins

Blend first 4 ingredients, add all dry ingredients & stir. Melt solid all vegetable shortening in frying pan to fill pan to 1½". Drop dough by teaspoonfuls into hot shortening & fry for 2-3 min. or till brown. Drain on paper towels. Place coatings (either powdered sugar or a mixture of ¼ c sugar & ½ t cinnamon) in paper bags & shake till coated. These are easy & kids love to make them!

Grace Merrill
Naperville

CHOCOLATE CHIP DIP

8   oz. pkg. cream cheese
½   stick butter
¼ c sugar
a sprinkle of cinnamon
a shake of nutmeg
1   t vanilla

Cream butter & cream cheese. Add all ingredients. Stir in small pkg. of chocolate chips. Add raisins if desired. Serve with graham crackers. Great for children's party.

Denise Bell
Schaumburg

CREAM CHEESE MINTS

1   3 oz. pkg. cream cheese
3   c   powdered sugar
mint flavoring to taste
food coloring - your choice

Mix all together well. Roll into tiny balls & press criss cross with cold
fork. (If fork sticks you need more powdered sugar.) Refrigerate for firmness. Great for wedding showers, baby showers, parties, etc.

Denise Bell
Schaumbug

ROCKY ROAD CANDY

1   12 oz. pkg. chocolate chips
1   14 oz. can of sweetened condensed milk
2   T butter or margarine
1   10½ oz. pkg. of tiny marshmallows
1   8 oz. jar of peanuts

Combine the first 3 ingredients in pan & cook over low heat till chocolate melts. Combine the last 2 ingredients in large bowl, add the chocolate mixture. Line a 9x13 pan with waxed paper & spread mixture evenly. Chill for 2 hours in freezer. Cut in squares or cut into pieces.

Ann Bagley
Naperville

"KOOKIE" BRITTLE

1   c   margarine
1½ t   vanilla
1   t   salt
1   c   sugar
2   c   flour
1   6 oz. pkg. chocolate chips
1   c   finely chopped nuts

Blend well; margarine, vanilla, salt. Gradually beat in sugar. Add flour, chocolate chips & ¾ c nuts, mix well. Press evenly into ungreased 10x15 pan. Sprinkle rest of nuts over. Bake at 375° for 25 min. or till golden brown. Cool then break in irregular pieces.

MaryAnn O'Brien
Frankfort

BUTTERY CINNAMON SKILLET APPLES

⅓ c butter
½ to ¾ c sugar
2   T cornstarch
1½ c water
¼ to ½ t cinnamon
4   medium apples, cored, unpeeled & halved

In skillet melt butter over med. heat. Stir in sugar & cornstarch & mix well. Add remaining ingredients. Cover & cook spooning sauce over apples occasionally till apples are fork tender & sauce is thick. (12-15 min.) Yields 4 servings or 2 c sauce.

MaryAnn O'Brien
Frankfort

OREO ICE CREAM

3   egg yolks
1   can Eagle Brand milk
1   c   coarsely crushed Oreo cookies
4   t   vanilla
2   t   water
2   8 oz. cartons whipping cream, whipped

In large bowl, beat egg yolks. Stir in Eagle Brand milk, vanilla & water.
Fold in whipped cream & Oreo crumbs. Pour into aluminum foil lined 9x5
loaf pan or any 2 qt. casserole dish. Freeze till solid.

Carol Miles
Elmhurst

HOME MADE CARMEL CORN

- 2 c packed dark brown sugar
- 1 c butter
- ½ c light corn syrup
- 1 t salt
- 1 T vanilla
- 1 t baking soda
- 7½ qts. popped corn (approx. 1 c unpopped corn)

Mix sugar, butter, corn syrup & salt in a heavy saucepan. Heat till boiling & boil 5 min., stirring often. Add baking soda, then add vanilla, mixing thoroughly. Place popped corn in a large aluminum baking pan & pour carmel sauce over stirring to coat evenly. Bake at 200° for one hour, stirring every 15 min. to assure even coating. Cool & eat!

Jack Kielczynski
LaGrange

POPCORN SNACKS

Chocolate Mint Popcorn: Heat butter & add 4-6 chocolate covered mint patties. When melted pour over popped corn.

Sugar & Spice Popcorn: Add 2 or 3 T sugar, ¼ t cinnamon & ¼ t nutmeg to butter. Stir till sugar is dissolved. Toss with popped corn.

Nancy Suffolk
Glendale Heights

COOKING NATURALLy

Herb Garden

W. SUFFOLK

NUTRITIOUS, DELICIOUS, "SHAKE & BAKE" CHICKEN

Remove skin from chicken pieces.

Place in a plastic bag:

½ c **bran**
½ c **wheat germ**
2 T **dried parsley**
¾ t **garlic powder**
¾ t **onion powder**
2 T **dried onion**
salt & pepper

Shake 2 or 3 pieces of chicken at a time in bag & place in baking dish. (No extra grease in pan.) Sprinkle parmesan cheese over. Bake at 350° for 1 hour.

Grace Merrill
Naperville

SUMMERTIME GARDENER'S LASAGNA

6   c   sliced zucchini
½   #   ground beef (opt.)
1   clove garlic, minced
8   oz. tomato sauce
1   t   salt
¼   t   oregano
¼   t   basil
1   c   small curd cottage cheese
1   egg, beaten
1   T   parsley flakes
¼   c   dry bread crumbs
1   c   shredded mozzarella cheese

Cook zucchini till crisp-tender, drain. Cook beef & garlic till beef browned, stir in tomato sauce, salt, oregano & basil. Blend cottage cheese, egg & parsley in another bowl. Put ½ of zucchini in greased 8″ sq. baking dish. Sprinkle with ½ the bread crumbs. Spread with ½ the cottage cheese mixture, then ½ the beef mixture & ½ the mozzarella. Repeat layers but reserve the remaining mozzarella until lasagna is almost done, then sprinkle on, put in oven & bake till cheese melts. Bake at 350° for 45 min. or till hot & bubbly. (I double recipe & put in 9x13 pan.)

Diane O'Conner
Downers Grove

VEGETARIAN CASSEROLE

1   med. onion, chopped
1   sm. green pepper, chopped
2   c noodles, cooked & drained
1½ c shredded monterey jack cheese
1   c broccoli cuts, cooked & drained
1   c sliced carrots, cooked & drained
1   c sliced zucchini, cooked & drained
½ c milk
¾ t salt
⅛ t pepper
1   stalk celery, chopped

Cook celery, onion & green pepper in hot oil till tender, stir in noodles, cheese, vegetables, milk, salt & pepper. Turn into greased 1½ qt. casserole. Bake covered at 350° for 15 min. Combine ¼ c fine bread crumbs, 2 T shredded cheddar, 1 T wheat germ & T melted butter & sprinkle around edge of dish. Bake uncovered 10 min. or till hot & bubbly. (I like to use ½ whole wheat or spinach noodles & ½ regular.)

Bonnie Lovison
Chicago

SUPERBURGERS WITH ZUCCHINI & CHEESE

¾ # lean ground beef
¾ c toasted wheat germ
salt & pepper
¼ c minced onion
½ t oregano
¼ t thyme
¼ c milk
5 med. zucchini, sliced
2 T oil
8 oz. tomato sauce
1 8 oz. pkg. mozzarella cheese, sliced

Mix beef, wheat germ, 1 t salt, pepper to taste & onion, oregano, thyme & milk. Form into 8 small flat patties. Brown in oiled skillet, turning once, set aside. Saute zucchini in skillet till tender, sprinkle with salt. Layer zucchini, meat patties & tomato sauce in 1½ qt. baking dish. Top with sliced mozzarella cheese & bake at 375° for 25-30 min.

Diane O'Connor
Downers Grove

FRUIT STRATA SALAD

3   c   shredded lettuce
1   honeydew melon, peeled, seeded & cubed
1   20 oz. can pineapple chunks, drained
1   pt. strawberries, halved
1   large banana, sliced
1   8 oz. carton pineapple, lemon or vanilla yogurt
½   c   shredded gruyere or swiss cheese

In large bowl place ½ of lettuce. Layer fruits atop lettuce. Top with remaining lettuce. Spread yogurt next & sprinkle with cheese. Cover & chill 2-3 hours. If desired, garnish with a few strawberry halves & fresh mint. Toss gently, serves 12.

Mary Wilson
Wheaton

MUSHROOM HEALTH SALAD

1   lg. head leaf lettuce
2   c bean sprouts, rinsed
½   # each: sliced swiss cheese & mushrooms
½   c each: toasted sliced almonds & plain yogurt
1   t oil
½   t dillweed
⅛   t salt
⅛   t garlic powder

Layer in large salad bowl, torn lettuce leaves, bean sprouts, sliced mushrooms, swiss cheese cut in 3″ strips & top with toasted almonds. For dressing combine yogurt, dill, oil, salt & garlic powder with a whisk. Pour over salad & toss just before serving.

Diane O'Connor
Downers Grove

BULGUR PILAF

1   c   bulgur, dry, cracked, unseasoned
½   t   salt
¼   c   chopped onion
¼   c   chopped green pepper
2   T   butter
2   c   chicken or beef broth
1   4 oz. can mushrooms
¼   t   thyme

Place onions & peppers in pan & saute in butter. Put in bulgur & coat with the butter. Add broth, mushrooms & thyme & place in one qt. casserole. Bake at 350° for 30-40 min.

Nancy Foerster
Downers Grove

BROWN RICE WITH WATER CHESTNUTS

1   c   brown rice
2   T   butter
2½   c   boiling water
2-3   chicken or beef bouillon cubes
¼   t   pepper
4   green onions, minced
1   c   sliced mushrooms
1   8 oz. can water chestnuts, drain & slice
1   2 oz. jar pimento, chopped

Saute rice in butter stirring constantly for 3 min. Add boiling water, bouillon cubes, pepper & onions. Heat to boil, reduce heat & cook covered over low heat for 45 min. or till rice is tender. Stir in mushrooms, water chestnuts & pimento, cook just till heated & adjust seasonings if needed.

Diane O'Connor
Downers Grove

WHOLE-WHEAT BANANA BREAD

1	c	mashed bananas
2		eggs beaten
½	c	shortening melted
1	c	whole wheat flour
¾	c	unbleached flour
¾	c	sugar
1	t	baking powder
¾	t	salt
½	t	baking soda
½	c	chopped nuts (optional)
½	c	raisins or chopped dates (optional)

Mix well bananas, eggs & shortening. In large bowl, mix well flours, sugar, powder, salt & soda. Stir in banana mixture just to blend. Add raisins & nuts if desired. Bake in a well greased 9x5 loaf pan at 350°, for 1 hour or till toothpick comes out clean. Cool in pan on rack 10 min., remove from pan & cool completely.

Donna Doherty
Merrillville

BANANA-ORANGE BREAD OR MUFFINS

1   c   flour
½   c   whole wheat flour
½   c   bran
1   c   sugar
½   c   oil
1½   c   mashed banana
¼   c   orange marmalade
2   beaten eggs
1   t   baking soda
¼   t   salt
¼   c   each: chop. nuts & unsweetened coconut

In bowl combine sugar & oil, blend in bananas, orange marmalade & eggs. Stir together flours, bran, soda & salt & stir into banana mixture. Stir in nuts & coconut. Bake in greased loaf pans either (1) 9x5 or (2) 7x3's. Also can be made into muffins, fill 12 muffin papers ⅔. Bake at 375°, 30-40 min. for breads or 20 min. for muffins.

Diane O'Connor
Downers Grove

BANANA DATE MUFFINS

1   c   unbleached flour
½   c   whole wheat flour
2   t   baking powder
¼   t   baking soda
1   c   mashed bananas
⅓   c   oil
¾   t   salt
½   c   sugar
1   c   chopped dates
1   egg

Sift flours, powder & soda into bowl. Mix bananas, beaten egg, oil, salt & sugar. Pour banana mixture into flour & mix again, only till ingredients are moistened. Fold in dates. Fill 12 muffin papers ⅔ full. Bake at 400° for 25-30 min.

Diane O'Connor
Downers Grove

GRANOLA-RASPBERRY BARS

CRUMB MIXTURE
1   c   unbleached flour   ⅓   c   sugar
¼   c   whole wheat   ½   c   butter

FILLING
½   c   raisins   ½-¾ c   raspberry (or any kind)
                                           preserves

TOPPING
¼   c   honey   ⅓   c   unsweetened coconut
2   T   butter   ⅓   c   sunflower seeds
¾   c   oats   2   T   sesame seeds

In bowl mix all crumb mixture till crumbly. Press onto bottom of greased 7x11 pan. Bake at 350° for 20 min. or till edges are browned. In same bowl combine all filling ingredients & stir. In 2 qt. pan combine honey & butter & cook till smooth, stir in other topping ingredients. To assemble: spread filling over hot crust, spoon topping mixture over filling & spread evenly. Bake for 15-20 minutes or till edges are browned. Cool & cut in bars.

Mary Wilson
Wheaton

OATMEAL CHIP COOKIES

1½	c	sugar
1	c	butter or margarine
1		egg
¼	c	water
1	t	vanilla
1¼	c	flour
¼	c	wheat germ
½	c	sunflower seeds
½	t	baking soda
½	t	salt
3	c	oatmeal
6		oz. carob or chocolate chips

Blend sugar, margarine, egg, water & vanilla till smooth. Stir in remaining ingredients. Drop dough by teaspoonfuls onto ungreased cookie sheet. Bake at 350° for 10-12 min. or till lightly browned.

Nancy Foerster
Downers Grove

WHOLE WHEAT OATMEAL COOKIES

1 c   butter or margarine
1 c   packed brown sugar
2 t   vanilla
¼ t   salt
⅔ c   raisins, carob or chocolate chips
2½ c oatmeal
1¼ c whole wheat flour
1 t   baking soda

In large bowl cream butter, sugar, vanilla & salt till fluffy. Stir in raisins, then oats till well blended (use hands if necessary). Use a teaspoonful & form into round cookies. Place on ungreased cookie sheet & bake at 325° for 20-25 min. or till light brown. Cool on rack.

Denise Bell
Schaumburg

HONEY NUTTERS

1   c   peanut butter
⅔   c   honey
½   c   instant non-fat dry milk
16   crushed graham crackers
toasted wheat germ

Mix well peanut butter, honey, dry milk & graham crackers. Shape into small balls & roll in toasted wheat germ. Keep covered in refrigerator.

Mary Wilson
Wheaton

CRUNCHY PEANUT BUTTER COOKIES

2   c   flour
1   t   baking soda
½   t   salt
¾   c   margarine
1   c   white sugar
½   c   brown sugar
2   eggs
¾   c   crunchy peanut butter
1   t   vanilla
1   c   oats

Beat margarine & sugars till smooth. Beat in eggs. Add dry ingredients & blend well. Make into small balls & flatten with fork. Bake at 375° for 8-10 min.

Denise Bell
Schaumburg

CAROB-PEANUT BUTTER CRISPS

2   c   carob chips
1   c   peanut butter
2½ c   wheat nuts (buy in health food store)

In double boiler, melt chips & peanut butter till smooth. Add wheat nuts & mix well. Can either press mixture on bottom of 9x13 foil lined pan or put into mini muffin papers & chill till solid. Cut pan into squares.

Mary Wilson
Wheaton

SIMPLE GRAHAM CRACKER DESSERT

14   graham crackers
3   eggs
1   c brown sugar
1   c chopped nuts
1   t baking powder
½   c dates chopped

Crumble the crackers & mix everything together. Put in greased pan & bake 15 min. Raisins & other dried fruit may also be added or substituted.

Sue Hofmann
Westmont

LO-CAL CHEESECAKE PIE

16   oz. low fat cottage cheese
1 T lemon juice
3   eggs
½ c each: sugar & skim milk
1 t vanilla
graham cracker 9″ crust
fresh sliced fruit

Combine the cheese & lemon juice in blender or processor till smooth. Beat eggs with sugar in large bowl. Add cheese mixture, milk & vanilla & beat till smooth. Pour into prepared graham cracker crust & bake at 350° for 45 min. or till set. Cool & chill. Spread top with sliced fresh fruit of your choice.

Judy Oslack
Downers Grove

BLUEBERRY FLUMMERY

This is a super simple & attractive dessert!

2   T cornstarch
½   c sugar
2¼ c blueberries
grated rind & juice of 1 lemon

Combine cornstarch & sugar. Stir in 1½ c water & blueberries, lemon rind & juice. Cook on low heat, stirring till bubbly & thickened. Spoon into sherbet glasses & chill. Can be topped with whipped cream.

Judy Oslack
Downers Grove

KNOX NATURE BLOX

Better for you than regular Knox Blox - less sugar & more nutritious.

4   env. unflavored gelatin
2 c apple yogurt
½ c apple juice
1 c boiling water
¼ c honey
½ c chopped nuts or raisins

In large bowl sprinkle gelatin over apple juice, add boiling water & stir till completely dissolved. With whisk or beater, blend in yogurt & honey. Pour into 8″ or 9″ square pan & sprinkle with nuts & raisins. Chill till firm. Makes 5-6 dozen squares. (Can use other juices & fruit yogurts.)

Sue Hofmann
Westmont

PUDDING POPSICLES

2   c   milk
1   can of Milnot
1   sm. pkg. instant pudding (any kind)

Mix all ingredients with a rotary beater for 2 minutes. Put into popsicle holders & freeze.

Cindi McCabe
Downers Grove

FROZEN STRAWBERRY-YOGURT POPS

1	c	fresh or frozen unsweetened strawberries
1	c	plain yogurt
5	T	honey
7		3½ oz. paper or plastic cups
7		wooden popsicle sticks

Blend strawberries till smooth, add yogurt & honey & mix well. Pour mixture into cups, fill about ⅔ full. Put a wooden stick in each. Freeze.

Another super simple, nutritious idea is: In processor or blender put 1 large can fruit, any kind, & blend till smooth. Pour into popsicle holders or cups with wooden sticks & freeze. So much better than the store bought, artificial flavor & color kind.

Sue Hofmann
Westmont

EASY YOGURT DESSERTS

YOGURT PUDDING
Combine ¼ c sugar & 1 env. of unflavored gelatin. In sm. pan heat ½ c milk till just boiling & pour into blender. Add sugar mix, cover & blend 2 min. to dissolve gelatin. Through hole in lid add 6 ice cubes one at a time till smooth. Add fruit yogurt of your choice, plus ½ - 1 c of any chopped fresh fruit. Blend till smooth. Pour into dishes & chill. Sprinkle with almonds if desired.

YOGURT PARFAITS
In 6 parfait glasses put a little plain yogurt into bottom. Top with some crushed pineapple, sprinkle chopped nuts & a drizzle of honey. Top with more yogurt & garnish with strawberries. Refrigerate till serving time.

Denise Bell
Schaumburg

APRICOT BREAKFAST SWIRL

2	c	milk
2		eggs
½	c	cream style cottage cheese
8¾		oz. can apricot halves, chilled
1	T	sugar
1	t	vanilla

In blender combine milk, eggs, cottage cheese, undrained apricots, sugar & vanilla. Blend till smooth. If desired add 1 or 2 ice cubes to chill. Makes 5 servings.

Nancy Suffolk
Glendale Heights

FRESH FRUIT DRINKS

STRAWBERRY-PEACH DRINK
1   pt. strawberries, halved
1   16 oz. can peaches in lite syrup, drained
1   c yogurt
2   T wheat germ
honey & nutmeg to taste

Put all ingredients in blender or processor till smooth. Refrigerate 1 hr., garnish with whole strawberries. Makes 4-6 servings.

STRAWBERRY-ORANGE JUICE
2   c strawberries
2   c orange juice
3   T sugar

Puree all ingredients in blender or processor & chill. Serve over ice.

Judy Oslack
Downers Grove

NO-SUGAR FREEZER PEACH JAM

2   # ripe peaches, diced & peeled
½   t unflavored gelatin
2   T each: cold water & fresh lemon juice

Cook peaches in saucepan, stirring occasionally for 15 min., or till soft. Soften gelatin in 2 T cold water & let stand for 5 min. Mash fruit, stir in gelatin mixture & add lemon juice. Pour into freezer containers & freeze solid. Makes about 3 cups.

Betty Wedman
Hinsdale

GRANOLA

½ c **butter**
5 c **oats**
1½ c **coconut**
1 c **chopped almonds**
½ c **chopped walnuts**
½ c **sunflower seeds**
½ c **sesame seeds**
½ c **honey**
½ c **maple syrup**
½ c **apple juice**
2 c **raisins**

Melt butter & pour over oats. Add other dry ingredients & mix well. Heat honey, syrup & juice till well mixed. Pour over oat mixture & blend well. Put on large cookie sheet & bake at 275° for 2 hours. Watch corners & stir often. Add raisins last.

Judy Pease
Hinsdale

HOMEMADE, EASY & GOOD

HOMEMADE SWEETENED CONDENSED MILK

1	c	dry nonfat milk powder	⅓	c	boiling water
⅔	c	sugar	3	T	butter

Process all in blender till smooth & substitute in your favorite recipes.
Yields 1¼ c or 10 oz.

WHIPPED BUTTER

In processor put 1 # butter, cut up, 1¼ c water & ¾ c oil. Blend till
smooth, place in containers to freeze or refrigerate. 1 # butter or 2 c will
equal almost 4 c whipped.

WHIPPED TOPPING

6		ice cubes	2-3	T	sugar
½	c	dry milk powder	1	t	vanilla
¼	c	milk			

Process ice till crushed. Add other ingredients & blend till smooth &
fluffy. Serve immediately, good on pies, pudding or any dessert you wish.

Judy Pease
Hinsdale

Diane O'Connor
Downers Grove

HONEY-COCONUT SNACK

⅓   c   honey
¼   c   packed brown sugar
3   c   Total cereal
1   c   flaked or shredded coconut
1   c   slivered almonds

350° oven. Brush 15½ x 10⅓ x 1″ pan with softened margarine. Heat honey and brown sugar to boiling, stirring constantly; remove from heat. Add remaining ingredients until completely coated; spread in pan. Bake uncovered, stirring frequently for 10 minutes. After cooling for five minutes loosen with spatula. Let stand for 1 hour. Store in airtight container. Makes about six cups.

Irene McDonald
Downers Grove

BEST EVER VANILLA PUDDING

⅓ c sugar
¼ c corn starch
⅛ t salt
½-¾ c milk
1 t vanilla

Mix sugar, corn starch and salt. Add milk and bring to a boil, stirring constantly, for one minute. Remove from heat and stir in margarine and vanilla. Chill. Makes 2½ cups.

Diane O'Connor
Downers Grove

BAKED STUFFED PEARS

4   firm pears
2 T raisins
3 T chopped walnuts
1 T lemon juice
1 t honey
¼ c apple cider

Halve pears, remove seeds and core. Combine the raisins and walnuts and place in the hollowed-out pear halves. Mix together lemon juice, honey and cider and drizzle this over the stuffed pear halves. Dust with nutmeg and bake at 350°F for 30 min. Serve hot or cold with mounds of whipped dessert topping.

TOPPING INGREDIENTS
1 c ricotta cheese
1 T honey
¼ t vanilla extract

Place ricotta, honey and vanilla in blender on low speed until smooth. Chill. Ricotta can vary in consistency so if too thick to whip add a few tablespoons of milk.

Carol Miles
Elmhurst

GRAPES FANTASIA

1   c   yogurt
1   small banana
1   t   lemon juice
1   t   honey
dash of grated nutmeg
3   c   white seedless grapes, mint springs, garnish

Place the yogurt, banana, lemon juice, honey and nutmeg in a blender and process on low speed until smooth. Place grapes in serving bowl and pour yogurt mixture over top, garnish with mint sprigs. Serve chilled.

Pat Fortune
Elmhurst

SUMMER REFRESHERS

FROZEN GRAPES
Simply wash grapes and remove stems. Freeze in a single layer on a cookie sheet. When frozen, store in plastic container. Serve frozen or slightly defrosted so they will be juicier. Can be used as garnish for many desserts. Stock up when they are on sale!

FROZEN BANANA POPS
Peel bananas and secure in plastic wrap or foil. Place in the freezer until firm. For a variation, dip the bananas in yogurt and roll in coconut.

Bonnie Lovison
Downers Grove

INDEX

APPETIZERS & BEVERAGES *(Cont.)*

BREADS

SOUPS & SALADS

ENTREES

ENTREES *(Cont.)*

SWEETS

The Wee Cookbook
5602 Hillcrest Road
Downers Grove, IL 60516

Please send _____ copies of The Wee Cookbook @ $7.95 $_____
Plus postage and handling   @ $1.00 $_____
Illinois residents add 6¼% sales tax   @ $.50 $_____

Please make checks payable to The Irish Children's Fund.

Name _____

Address _____

City _____ State _____ Zip _____

— — — — — — — — — — — — — — — — — — — —

The Wee Cookbook
5602 Hillcrest Road
Downers Grove, IL 60516

Please send _____ copies of The Wee Cookbook @ $7.95 $_____
Plus postage and handling   @ $1.00 $_____
Illinois residents add 6¼% sales tax   @ $.50 $_____

Please make checks payable to The Irish Children's Fund.

Name _____

Address _____

City _____ State _____ Zip _____